AF322598

An Official Document Of
The Holy Reintegrated Church
&
The Mystical Order of the Nazarene

PARADISE TRANSCENDED

The Gospel of Gnosis and the Kingdom Within

Elder Zimriah Ex LUX Aeturnus

Table Of Contents

The Veiled Eden and the Flame Within

Beloved seeker of hidden Light, a question ancient as the breath of God arises and abides: How shall the soul know the Way, the Truth, and the Life? This inquiry proceeds not from contention nor from the vanity of accumulation, but from the stillness wherein the Holy Spirit begets remembrance, and from that depth the Logos Himself addresses the mind with authority.

The Lord proclaims: "I am the way, the truth, and the life: no man cometh unto the Father, but by me." (John 14:6) In this utterance the veil is parted and the eternal order is manifested: the Way is the procession of the Only-Begotten from the bosom of the Unbegotten into the realm of our pilgrimage; the Truth is the radiant self-disclosure of the Invisible Father in the face of the Son; the Life is the uncreated Light by whom all being subsists and in whom the mortal breath is ordained toward immortality. Thus, the confession of the Church is simple and entire: to behold the Son is to be set upon the Way, to be illuminated by the Truth, and to be quickened into the Life.

This confession summons the soul from opinion to contemplation and from contemplation to obedience, for knowledge in Christ is not a hoarded possession but a participation in His procession and return. The question, therefore, becomes a seal upon the heart, impressing a form of reverent attention by which the intellect is purified, the memory is awakened, and the will is directed toward the Good.

And because the divine economy orders all things from first things to last, this same question prepares the pattern of our ascent: Eden is unveiled as the place of custody and probation; the Cross is manifest as the descent of Light into our bonds; the Kingdom is disclosed within as the rule of Christ over the renewed heart; and the Tree of Life is recognized as Christ Himself, by whom the exile is ended and communion restored. In this order, the reader is made ready to consider Eden as it truly stands before the cherubic flame, to behold the medicine of the Cross, to receive the interior reign of the King, and to taste in hope the everlasting Fruit.

Therefore, let the faithful receive this question as a sacred charge and a lamp of doctrine: the Way is the manifested procession of the Logos, the Truth is the Father's radiance in the Son, and the Life is the uncreated Light communicated by the Spirit unto deification. Having confessed thus, the mind is prepared to pass to the veiling of Eden and the beginning of our ascent.

On the Veiling of Eden

Eden abides within the human memory as a form impressed upon the soul, a first pattern by which origin, transgression, and the narrative of banishment are contemplated; and though many reduce it to an infantile allegory or a dispute of historians, the Church receives it as a mysterious beginning whose imprint still governs desire and judgment. In this figure, the Lord manifests both His goodness and His order, for whatever the ages distort, the primordial seal remains.

The remembrance of Eden is given beneath a veil. The prohibition signifies illumination reserved for maturity; the removal from the Garden establishes a pedagogy of mercy; the flaming sword is a liturgy of protection by which immortality is withheld until the creature is capacitated for glory. Thus, the economy is preserved: wisdom is not denied but prepared; life is not confiscated but safeguarded; the sanctuary is not erased but concealed for a time within the chambers of the soul.

This veiling belongs to the divine philanthropy. The Father appoints seasons; the Logos proclaims the order of ascent; the Spirit interiorly disposes of the heart to remembrance. In this light, Eden is known as a sanctuary hidden within, awaiting disclosure by repentance and illumination. When the veil is lifted, one perceives that the Garden's boundaries instruct the will, that the cherubic ministry guards the sacred, and that the Tree is preserved for a consummation that Christ alone bestows.

Such understanding prepares the reader for the first inquiry of this work. Chapter I shall consider the Garden as a place of custody under a rule that disciplines the creature, so that the Cross may be recognized as the descent of Light into our bonds, the Kingdom as the interior reign of the Son within the obedient heart, and the Tree of Life as Christ Himself communicated to the faithful.

Eden stands as a veiled sanctuary instituted in mercy, its guard a prudent pedagogy, its Tree preserved for deification; and the unveiling proceeds according to the order of salvation, first the discipline of the Garden, then the medicine of the Cross, thereafter the Kingdom within, and at last participation in the Tree of Life, who is Christ our Lord.

On the Path of Gnosis in Christ

A revelation entered the world whose radiance the darkness could not master, for the Logos manifested in flesh and silenced the ancient shadow by His Light. This manifestation stands above philosophy and beyond sect, unveiling the mystery hidden before the ages and now present in the Person of the Only Begotten.

The Lord came as righteousness embodied, and wisdom proclaimed, He ordered doctrine toward participation and disciplined conduct toward deification. His advent was the rending of the veil and the opening of what had been closed, for He declared the nearness of the Kingdom and bestowed its power through His own obedience unto the Cross. Thus, the Gospel is first a divine act and only then a teaching: the Son manifests the Father, the veil is parted by the Passion, and the way of return is established in the Spirit.

Concerning this Kingdom, the Lord speaks, "Neither shall they say, Lo here! or, lo there! for, behold, the kingdom of God is within you." (Luke 17:21), and by this utterance He appoints the interior throne from which He rules the renewed heart. The dominion of Christ is therefore known as an indwelling reality: the Invisible Father is acknowledged through the Son's radiance, and the Spirit disposes the soul to receive the rule of the King within.

Gnosis in Christ is the remembrance and participation granted by grace: a knowing that becomes being, a light that orders the mind, a life that conforms the will to the Good. It precedes words in its origin and perfects words in its fruit, for the same Logos who undergirds true doctrine grants illumination to comprehend it. Where the mind cleaves to Him, knowledge matures into wisdom and faith flowers into sight.

The Gospel written bears witness to the Gospel manifested, and the Gospel manifested grants the fullness of what is written. In this order, the Church confesses one mystery: the Word proclaimed in Scripture is the Word who indwells the faithful, and by His Light the soul is led from the discipline first learned at Eden, through the medicine of the Cross, into the interior Kingdom, and onward to the Tree of Life who is Christ Himself.

The path of gnosis is participation in the manifested Logos: the Cross opens the veil, the Kingdom is enthroned within, and the same Light conducts the faithful toward consummation in the Fruit of the Tree of Life, even our Lord Jesus Christ.

On the Call to Remembrance

Wherever the Light is proclaimed, disputation accompanies its appearing, for the mystery precedes the tongue and exceeds the measure of creeds. Gnosis in Christ is participation rather than possession: the Spirit awakens remembrance, the Logos inscribes wisdom within the obedient heart, and the Father manifests His goodness through this interior illumination.

Across the ages, many who confess the Name have treated gnosis as a rival camp or a private store, yet the Church discerns it as the interior fruit of the same Gospel that is preached aloud. The writings testify, the sacraments nourish, and the Spirit grants understanding; in this order, knowledge matures into wisdom and faith advances toward sight. Gnosis remains Christic in source and ecclesial in form, for the Light that enlightens is the Light that gathers, and the remembrance bestowed is ordered to charity and obedience.

Those who traffic in symbols without the Logos fall into abstraction; those who trumpet doctrine without illumination weary the soul with recitation. The healing of this fracture is given from above: the Son manifests the Truth, the Cross opens the veil, the Kingdom is enthroned within, and the Spirit restores the memory of our origin and end. Thus, the discipline learned at Eden is recognized as pedagogy, the Passion as medicine, and the interior reign as the governance that disposes the soul for communion with the Tree of Life.

The call that follows is therefore a summons to anamnesis. Remembrance is the form of true knowledge, for the same Light that fashioned the heart renews it; the same Wisdom that ordered the aeons orders the mind; the same Charity that created all things perfects all things in the saints. In this remembrance, the Church learns to confess with understanding, to contemplate with purity, and to walk with a will conformed to the Good.

Gnosis is the restoration of memory in the Spirit, the illumination of the mind by the Logos, and the ordering of the heart under the Father's Kingdom; by this remembrance the faithful advance from the discipline of Eden through the medicine of the Cross toward the interior reign of Christ, and are made ready for the foretaste of Paradise in the Fruit of the Tree of Life.

On the Foretaste of Paradise

This work is ordered for transformation and disposed toward illumination; it awakens the memory implanted by the Spirit before the courses of the ages and shapes the mind for participation in the divine Life. Its pages stand as thresholds and its chapters as gates, instructing that they may transfigure, and teaching that the learner may advance from knowledge to wisdom and from wisdom to charity.

The operation of grace is quiet and efficacious. While the Word is received, the hidden Light once enclosed manifests within the obedient heart. The doctrine proposed is a seed of the Logos cast into sacred soil; the Spirit grants increase according to season, until understanding ripens into the love that perfects all things. Thus, instruction becomes medicine, remembrance becomes strength, and contemplation becomes praise.

Such ordering accords with the divine economy. First, the reader is prepared to behold Eden under its veil of mercy; then the Cross is confessed as the rending of that veil and the medicine of our wounds; thereafter, the Kingdom is recognized as the interior reign of Christ over the renewed heart; and at last the Tree of Life is tasted as Christ Himself communicated to the faithful. The whole movement proceeds from figure to fulfillment, from pedagogy to communion, from exile to deification.

Therefore, the fruit offered here is a foretaste. It is given as a pledge of the Spirit and an earnest of the age to come, so that what is apprehended in doctrine is possessed in life, and what is contemplated in prayer is consummated in charity. Those who receive this order learn to think with the Church, to love in the Spirit, and to walk under the yoke of the Logos until the soul becomes a temple of uncreated radiance.

Receive this invitation with reverence. The way set forth is interior, the guide is the manifested Logos, and the end is participation in the uncreated Light. Let seekers of scattered wisdom be anchored in Him who precedes all beginnings and remains beyond all endings; let knowledge be ordered to remembrance, remembrance to illumination, and illumination to charity.

Discern also the antiquity of this wisdom. Truth abides before our partitions, and the seeds of revelation are preserved by Providence for their appointed hour. The Logos, proceeding from the Unbegotten, governs the seasons of disclosure; Sophia, His radiant wisdom, disposes the heart to receive what is given. In this order, doctrine serves participation, and contemplation matures into obedience.

Behold Christ in His fullness: the Word by whom all things subsist and the Light who indwells every soul. He instructs unto righteousness, He heals by His Passion, and He reigns within by His Spirit; the mind is enlightened, the will is strengthened, and desire is directed toward the Good.

This summons is to Truth unveiled and to repentance as conversion from ignorance to knowledge, from dispersion to integrity, from banishment to filial rest. The seed is cast by teaching, the growth is given by grace, and the fruit is deification, that the soul may become a temple of radiance and a participant in the life it confesses.

In consenting to this order, the reader is disposed for the ascent: Eden is unveiled in mercy, the Cross rends the veil, the Kingdom is enthroned within, and the Tree of Life, who is Christ Himself, is approached in communion.

What is given here is also sowing for days to come. A beginning is planted that shall bear fruit in times appointed by the Father: hints of deeper studies, signs toward further works, and foundations laid for the path that leads from exile to deification. Sown in humility and watered in contemplation, these seeds, in their season, yield wisdom and virtue, until the soul is transfigured into a temple of uncreated Light. Let them take root in the silent soil of the spirit, under the gentle rain of Sophia's wisdom and the warming Light of the Logos, that they may grow into trees whose fruit nourishes and whose leaves heal.

Before the gate, let prayer seal the heart:

The Emanator's Prayer

Emanator of living Light, shine in us and show us the Way.

Return us to Your Oneness through our fiery hearts and willing
hands;
Make our desires align with Yours.
Give us this day Gnosis and bread, for we are not sustained on
bread alone.
Unbind us from our guilt as we unbind others from our blame.
Let us not be forgetful or forgotten, but free us from naivete.
From You came sovereignty, discipline, and the poetic beauty
of life that was, is, and is to come.
May these words be our nature sealed in trust, faith, and truth.
Amen.

This book ministers a foretaste of Paradise: by the
illumination of the mind, the strengthening of the will, and the
ordering of desire, it conducts the faithful along the ascent
Eden unveiled, the Cross confessed, the Kingdom enthroned
within unto communion with the Tree of Life, who is Christ
our Lord.

Therefore, let the reader enter with reverence, for this
work unfolds as an ascent: from Eden unveiled, through the
Cross wherein Light descends, unto the Kingdom within, and
at last to the Tree of Life, which is Christ Himself. Paradise is
not behind us in memory, but before us in fulfillment.

Chapter One

The Garden Was a Prison

Eden stood adorned in fruitfulness and abundance, its order decreed upon the silent soil by the command of Yahweh. Here, in this theological reading, the craftsman is distinguished in Gnostic witnesses from the Unbegotten Father. Beneath its manifold beauty, there abided a mystery veiled from sight, for what appeared as perfection to the senses disclosed an incompleteness awaiting the manifestation of true being beyond splendour.

Adam was positioned at the midst of this unmoving domain, his soul unquickened, his form upright yet constrained in spirit. Life was fashioned to surround him as an adornment rather than to participate with him in divine fellowship. At the heart of this enclosure were appointed two trees: one bearing life, the other knowledge; the latter alone was proscribed, and their very placement determined the boundary that rendered the deception complete.

Christian and Hebrew tradition has proclaimed Eden as paradise; the ancient Gnostic testimony discerns a carceral order established by a subordinate power intent upon enclosing the hidden potential of divinity within man. As the Apocryphon of John, consonant with apostolic proclamation in its zeal to unveil the rulers, bears witness, this power is named Yaldabaoth, a ruler without rest in the Fullness, a derivative emission arising through Sophia's disorder, who asserts a sovereignty he does not possess.

Yaldabaoth is barren of true generative power. He arranges the elements of matter into the likeness of order, fashioning imitations of realities he cannot comprehend. His garden manifests a covering cast over the soul, obscuring the memory of its origin; he delineates boundaries and calls them blessings, establishes constraints and names them goodness, bestows outward delights that appease the senses while withdrawing nourishment from the spirit.

Genesis bears witness to a "LORD God" who formed man from the dust and breathed into him; yet the same tradition confesses more deeply that the Archons, as extensions of the Demiurge, shaped the form of Adam's body, and their breath proved impotent to impart life. Only the Spirit descending from beyond the Fullness, from the realm of the Hidden God, entered that form and stirred it unto living being.

Therefore, let it be confessed in sober doctrine: being proceeds from the Father, the Unbegotten Source, whose efflux sustains all things and in whose generosity, creation stands; governance within Eden, however, is administered under a usurped economy, for the Demiurge with his ministers imposes a counterfeit polity upon the garden. In the mystery signified by Yesod, the Father's overflow upholds the creature, while within the enclosed precinct, the archonic order asserts its alien rule;

thus, subsistence descends from the Highest even as administration within Eden remains disordered.

Eden thus functions as a construction of containment, a simulated sanctuary that silences inquiry and suppresses spiritual memory. The Garden presents an image of sanctity without the communion that illumines and purifies; it offers rest to the senses while deferring the soul's ascent toward its Principle.

Nevertheless, the order of concealment meets appointment with disclosure. In the midst, the Tree of Knowledge stands by necessity, for the light of truth presses toward manifestation. The fruit serves as a sacrament of revelation that transcends the bounded world; its partaking rends illusion and opens the first path of anamnesis, whereby spiritual memory awakens, and the exile begins to be recapitulated as pilgrimage toward the Light.

The Garden as a Construct of Control

Genesis situates the garden eastward in Eden and appoints it as the place wherein Adam is consigned "to dress it and to keep it" (Genesis 2:8–15). These verses manifest placement and duty rather than filial adoption or ontological vocation, for Adam's existence is rendered as a component within a designed enclosure whose beauty is ordered to the task at hand. "And out of the ground made the LORD God to grow every tree that is pleasant to the sight, and good for food;" (Genesis 2:9). Such loveliness rises before the gaze as an economy of appearances that captivates perception, while the deeper purpose of the soul awaits illumination from beyond the bounds of the garden. In this arrangement, we discern the abiding truth already confessed: subsistence proceeds from the Father's efflux, the foundational outflow that upholds all things, while the administration within Eden remains under an alien polity.

The revelations preserved within the Gnostic tradition, consonant with apostolic proclamation in their resolve to unmask the rulers, disclose the sinister cast of this design. Eden functions as a construction of containment, an arena wherein sensory delight is transmuted into spiritual sedation and where the faculties grow docile under a measured abundance. The Archons, fashioned by Yaldabaoth for jurisdiction over the lower domains, appear as artificers of forgetfulness, shaping a world in which the divine spark within humanity is held in abeyance; thus, Hypostasis of the Archons bears witness to a principality that structures ignorance as a regime.

These powers, named the Hebdomad, preside over the sevenfold spheres and bind the soul within the mechanism of the heavens. They fashion matter into a semblance of creation, constructing a prison whose veiled beauty dimly imitates the supernal brightness; their work echoes the Platonic shadow, for they operate in ignorance of the Forms and direct consciousness downward into mixture and decay rather than upward toward truth and life.

The Apocryphon of John deepens the matter and teaches that the rulers shaped Adam "according to the image," yet the power they bestowed could not set him upright nor animate him; through Sophia's compassionate intervention the spark descended by channels of the Fullness, and true Light entered the inert form as a gift that exceeds archonic capacity (Apocryphon of John, NH II,1; Meyer 2009). The episode does not display a derivative echo of their making; it manifests an intrusion of the higher economy, whereby the generosity of the Pleroma touches the clay and the image rises.

Hence, we discern that Eden does not bestow the life that animates humanity; it arranges a vessel whose ascension requires visitation from beyond. The breath confessed in Genesis descends from the ineffable Monad, beyond the reach of the rulers, and every feature of the garden, from rivers to trees, operates as a sensible boundary that trains the gaze to remain within the enclosure. The verb ʿābad (עבד) signifies service rendered under obligation, the labor of tilling and attending as a task imposed upon the earthbound steward. Likewise, shāmar (שמר) denotes vigilant guarding, a constant watch set over a charge, the posture of surveillance that maintains the precinct. Eden is thus ordered as a realm where obedience grounded in ignorance displaces the communion that illumines and purifies.

The prohibition "But of the tree of the knowledge of good and evil, thou shalt not eat of it: for in the day that thou eatest thereof thou shalt surely die." (Genesis 2:17) appears in the letter as a warning; in the unveiled reading, it functions as a containment decree whose design is to arrest the awakening of memory concerning the Fullness. Hypostasis recounts the visitation of the Instructor in serpentine form, who counsels the pair without fear and exposes the intention of the ban: lest they become as gods, knowing good and evil (Hypostasis of the Archons, NH II,4; Meyer 2009; cf. Genesis 3:5). The word thereby betrays its own strategy, for commandment is deployed as a hedge to preserve ignorance, and fear is invoked to keep the eyes from beholding what liberates.

Eden, therefore, stands as an oubliette adorned with delights: thresholds sealed by decree, walls clothed in radiance, appointments measured to detain the senses. The rivers serve as lines of division; the trees operate as instruments of enthrallment; the abundance functions as an inducement toward repose within appearances. Within this enclosure, the Archons orchestrate perception, mood, and thought, tethering the soul to a world they claim as final and directing the affections toward what passes away.

The cosmologies preserved in the Nag Hammadi corpus affirm the shape of this assault upon the soul. Yaldabaoth is depicted as lion-faced and serpentine-bodied, a malformed ruler whose dominion is sustained by distortion rather than truth; arrogance issues his decrees and ignorance perpetuates his throne, while memory is darkened so that the spark may lie dormant beneath the veil of images.

Yet hope abides within this architecture of captivity, for the spark endures and Light remains sovereign. The very prohibition draws the eye to the Tree, and the beauty of the place incites inquiry that exceeds its measure; thus, the Great Work emerges within the cage itself, and the silent sovereignty of the Monad converts the prison into a school of awakening. Even the strongest apparatus of the Demiurge becomes, under the hidden governance of the Highest, the field wherein holy revolt germinates and the first movements of liberation are rehearsed.

Having established this foundation, we now contemplate the Tree of Knowledge itself and behold how its hidden potency opened a breach in the demiurgic economy, inaugurating the soul's long recapitulation toward restoration.

The Tree of Knowledge and the Serpent

The Tree of Knowledge stood in the very center of Eden, vital in purpose and manifest in appearance, and it was sealed under decree. Its presence signaled intention beyond mortal reckoning. In much catechesis, it is treated as the cradle of transgression; in the unveiled economy of Gnosis, it is received as sacrament, for the tree opens the gate of recognition and its fruit administers wisdom from above, the first eucharist of remembrance within the narrative of awakening.

"In the day you eat of it, you shall surely die" (Genesis 2:17): the utterance asserts dominion and claims jurisdiction over the soul; it promulgates subjection rather than nurture and constrains consciousness from ascent into plenary awareness. When Eve partook and the eyes were opened, the serpent's word "For God doth know that in the day ye eat thereof, then your eyes shall be opened, and ye shall be as gods, knowing good and evil." (Genesis 3:5) found its confirmation in the text itself (Genesis 3:7); the veil thinned, and the image of truth began to appear. The prohibition functioned to preserve ignorance, because authority that is founded upon blindness trembles before illumination.

Consonant with apostolic proclamation in its resolve to unmask the rulers, Hypostasis of the Archons recounts that those who fashioned Adam's body became fearful when they perceived the Light stirring within him; they had shaped the form without power to animate it. The breath that entered descends from beyond, through the compassion of Christo-Sophia, by channels of the Pleroma; and with that inbreathing, the decline of archonic dominion commenced. The fruit of the Tree bears an analogous potency: it awakens remembrance of divine origin, a remembrance no counterfeit regime can endure.

The serpent speaks with clarity and discloses what had been concealed. In venerable Gnostic testimonies, he appears as the minister of Sophia, an instructor who reorients the gaze beyond imposed boundaries and restores attention to the realities that exceed the garden's design. In that moment, Eve recalls what surpasses the precinct and turns toward the Light that proceeds from the Father.

Yaldabaoth's rule persists through obscuration. His regime endures by the veil placed over spiritual origin, not by rightful sovereignty. Commandment is deployed as a hedge to interrupt recognition; fear becomes an instrument to arrest ascent. When Eve received the fruit, she returned to herself: mind, body, and soul were aligned once more toward their Source, and the counterfeit economy began to crumble under the pressure of unveiled memory.

Gnosis signifies the reawakening of the eternal remembrance implanted by the True God; it is Light recalled from on high and manifested anew by the Holy Spirit. Knowledge accompanies illumination as a faithful companion. To eat of the fruit marked a great turning: the eyes gained clarity, and the measure of spiritual authority within humanity was restored according to the dignity of the image.

In the mysteries of the Kabbalah, Daath is named as the hidden sefirah, the hush-point where the known stretches toward the ineffable and where image begins to pass into essence. The Tree of Knowledge fulfills this function with sacramental precision. Its fruit draws forth the Light already latent in the creature; each seed bears an echo of the Pleroma. This unveiling discloses a deeper dimension within the garden sexual mystery and generative vigor, which shall be expounded in due course in Chapter Four.

Eve acts with solemn conviction, and the narrative records a simple, unembellished sharing. She eats and the world alters; consciousness stirs, and the body, once veiled by imposed ignorance, becomes lucid and proportioned to its subtle faculties. This moment signals the first recognition that Adam and Eve were not standing before the Invisible Father; the soul reclaimed what had been planted within it from the beginning.

Eden's economy preserves separation. Rivers are appointed as lines of division. Trees serve as veils. Beauty pacifies the soul's holy longing. Law is proclaimed in a manner that denies ascent and distorts the righteous use of commandment. Within this regulated habitation, Eve's gesture calls Light into action, and her movement summons Adam into the same horizon.

Two conjectures fail upon the witness of Scripture. Ignorance is denied, for "And the eyes of them both were opened," (Genesis 3:7). Malice is excluded, for the fruit awakens moral recognition "and ye shall be as gods, knowing good and evil." (Genesis 3:5), and their first motion is modesty, not violence, as they gird themselves with leaves. The fitting reading prevails: Eve perceives truth and, moved by love, offers Adam the same awakening; for she is "bone of my bones, and flesh of my flesh" (Genesis 2:23), the companion through whom humanity advances together into knowledge. In the wisdom of the Gnostics, she stands as the first priestess of anamnesis, extending remembrance to the one from whom she was taken.

The Gospel of Truth attests a consonant mystery: when Truth appears, the world is troubled and its emanations recognize their Source. So too in Eden, recognition disturbs the counterfeit order and summons the image to return. The serpent's ministry remains plain: he calls forth remembrance, restores the soul's attention to the Highest, and exposes an illusion that had postured as finality.

The Tree of Knowledge abides as an emblem of awakening. The ancient interdiction echoes still through structures that suppress the divine spark; nevertheless, the fruit continues to impart its ancient gifts of remembrance, clarity, and the radiance that proceeds from the True God. The decree arose from a dominion founded in fear, while the soul is fashioned for ascent. By partaking, Adam and Eve transcended Eden's shadow and began the path of return to the Invisible Father, and thus the economy of exile already stirred toward pilgrimage under the quiet sovereignty of the Light.

The Psychology of a Prisoner

Eden restrained Adam and Eve by an architecture of conditioned perception, not through iron, but through a voice that projected power across the precinct, demarcated boundaries, and defined the terms of their existence. Command established their limits and threat set their consequences; a timorous apprehension took root within, wherein stillness masqueraded as safety and silence was esteemed as sanctity. The absence of discord was heralded as peace, while true peace is the presence of harmony ordered toward the divine. The garden stood meticulously arranged, and its order was maintained by a hand that exercised dominion beneath the canopy of delights; meanwhile, subsistence continued to proceed from the Father's efflux, that foundational outflow which upholds the creature even as governance within the enclosure shaped perception toward docility.

Such is the psychological foundation of captivity. Gnostically, it appears as the soul's descent into forgetfulness; anthropologically, it resembles what is now termed Stockholm Syndrome, wherein the captive begins to defend the very figure or structure that binds, especially when bondage is draped in order, aesthetic beauty, and the semblance of the sacred. In Eden, every contour of the precinct was clothed in perfection, yet each design served to inhibit ascent: rivers ordained division, fruit was withheld by edict, and the soul, kindled by divine fire, was instructed to avert its own Light.

The illusion of benevolence fortified dependence. The soul learned to count righteousness as trust in an external voice and to regard holy longing beyond the boundary as betrayal. The body, fashioned as a temple for the Light, was reframed as a vessel subject to another's jurisdiction. Consequently, obedience received the name of virtue, curiosity was branded as corruption, and inquiry was pacified with prohibitions. The very architecture of the garden interrupted the soul's upward motion. The Tree of Knowledge, set at the center, remained in paradox: visible to the sight and sealed by command, a source of wisdom presented before the gaze and rendered inaccessible by decree, an instrument contrived to arrest spiritual return.

At the heart of this order resounds the usurping voice, "I am the LORD, and there is none else, there is no God beside me." (cf. Isaiah 45:5; Apocryphon of John, NH II,1; Meyer 2009) Within Gnostic exegesis, such speech manifests insecurity and isolation rather than majesty: the proclamation of singularity issues from ignorance of the Fullness. Compulsion to silence competing testimony betrays a deeper fear that the soul might remember the True Father, whose utterance does not coerce but summons return, whose call purifies rather than subjugates.

Genesis records humanity's first reckoning with self-awareness: "I heard thy voice in the garden, and I was afraid, because I was naked; and I hid myself." And the voice answered, "Who told thee that thou wast naked?" (Genesis 3:10–11). These words inflicted the primal wound of the interior life. Vulnerability was exposed, and the power that had shaped Adam's world now named that exposure as failure; consciousness was made suspect at the very moment it opened its eyes.

Here begins shame as an implanted reaction at awakening, distinct from guilt. The soul beheld itself and was trained to recoil. Awareness was catalogued as an error. The body, created to be luminous with divine brilliance, was reinterpreted as something to be concealed. The desire to know received the mark of transgression, and that transgression was harvested by the system that established tree, prohibition, and penalty in a single economy of words.

Pathological shame entered as an instrument of rule. The soul interiorized its warden, enthroning a censor within, so that memory of the Origin would be stifled under the charge of disloyalty. The body, radiant with the spark of the Pleroma, was redefined as base material. Innocence was recast as scandal. The impulse to ascend was smothered before it could take form.

This distortion arises from ignorance. Consonant with apostolic proclamation, the Gospel of Truth teaches that loss proceeds from unknowing; sin is treated not as sheer lawlessness but as spiritual amnesia, the severing of the soul from its Principle. Humanity's crisis appears as the recognition of imprisonment within a world structured to suppress the Light. The fruit unveiled the architecture of captivity that dwelt beneath the language of sanctity and the theatre of ordered delight.

When knowledge entered, clarity followed; the veil of Eden began to dissolve. Exile ensued as the remaining recourse of a counterfeit dominion confronted by a soul that had begun to see, for any regime founded upon blindness collapses beneath the gaze of awakened eyes. Illumination pressed upon the whole edifice, and the soul was driven forth because it had remembered the Light it was never meant to recall.

Obedience within Eden secured confinement. The voice that instilled fear into self-awareness issued from one who imitates sovereignty and lacks generative power. The spark within humanity proceeds from a lineage beyond such jurisdiction; its movement toward remembrance fulfills its created design and recapitulates the creature toward its Source.

Beyond the garden's borders, the residue of captivity lingered. The voice of the precinct echoed in the interior depths; though awakened, the soul bore the impress of its former jailor. Self-deprecation shadowed the path. Shame clouded ascent. The fear of inquiry survived the dissolution of the walls. Across generations, the same whisper pursued the heirs of Adam: You are broken for asking; you are wrong for desiring more.

Yet the potency of that whisper wanes. Once the veil lifts, the soul interrogates what it had received without discernment: Who called this body shameful? Who declared anamnesis transgression? Who taught fear of the very Light enthroned within? Each question becomes an act of liberation, and the answers proceed from the Pleroma, the Fullness beyond all emanated realms. In the stillness that follows, Truth lives; the soul ceases to guard its captor, refuses to conceal the fire within, and abandons apology for beholding reality as it is. When that hour arrives, Eden remains behind as an enchantment broken, and the pilgrim steps forward under a sky made spacious by remembrance.

Divine Rejection or Demiurgic Retaliation?

Awakening dissolved the garden's efficacy. Eden lost its power through the waning of its necessity, for what once shimmered as paradise stood manifest as an apparatus of control. The precinct, shaped according to a limited artisanry, could no longer bind those who had remembered their origin; the spark within them had grown too luminous for the shadowed canopy.

Genesis recounts their removal, and the unveiled reading discerns the deeper cause: a calculated exile ordered to preserve a semblance of sanctity and to stabilize a counterfeit throne. The ruler expelled them in order to safeguard his economy, for the awakened presence threatened to unravel the order he had clothed in the language of divinity.

"Behold, the man is become as one of us, to know good and evil:" (Genesis 3:22). The phrase discloses the fear: likeness provoked alarm, for the illumined image mirrored the pattern he sought to imitate. Recognition, rather than mere transgression, occasioned his decree "and now, lest he put forth his hand, and take also of the tree of life, and eat, and live for ever:" (Genesis 3:22). The anxiety was clear: knowledge had begun, and consummation loomed.

Cherubim were then stationed, and a flaming sword set to turn every way, guarding the way to the Tree of Life (Gen. 3:24). The first tree had awakened sight; the second promised perfection. What had been displayed as ornament now appeared as the most guarded threshold within the lower creation.

This response reveals a tyrannical intent upon suppressing vision. The garden could not sustain those who discerned its nature, for its governance relied upon ignorance, upon beauty misread as goodness, upon silence mistaken for peace. When the spell of appearances broke, administrative exile remained the chosen instrument, an action crafted to remove sight from the precinct and to delay ascent.

What passed through the gate was capacity rather than corruption. The same Light that had animated Adam and the same discernment that had stirred within Eve now pressed against the whole fabric of the demiurgic order. The expulsion functioned as a last effort to arrest transformation and to halt the unveiling of an inefficacious throne.

Yet Providence revealed a paradox within the gesture. Exile became pilgrimage; displacement generated motion; the garden receded, and the soul stepped upon an earth unformed yet unbound. Beyond the borders, they were unsheltered, yet they were no longer imprisoned, for memory had already begun to lead them forward.

The promise of the Tree of Life endured and reappeared at the end of Scripture: "He that hath an ear, let him hear what the Spirit saith unto the churches; To him that overcometh will I give to eat of the tree of life, which is in the midst of the paradise of God." (Revelation 2:7), and again, the tree stands by the river, "which bare twelve manner of fruits," in its season (Revelation 22:2). The image is clear: what was guarded at the beginning flourishes unveiled at the consummation, set within the city where Light is its lamp.

In the economy of the Logos, what was sealed is opened and what was withheld is bestowed; access to Life is recapitulated as a gift. The tree once confined within a counterfeit paradise now blooms at the heart of a city radiant with the presence of the True God, and its fruit becomes the inheritance of those who persevere in remembrance.

The flaming sword continues its ministry, yet its purpose is understood as purification. The blade does not negate devotion; it refines seekers by cutting through illusion and by revealing what abides. The path remains guarded and also made passable for those who attend to the voice behind all commandments, to the God beyond all semblance, to the Light that transcends every emanation.

Thus, the narrative proceeds beyond the walls and beneath the unbounded sky. The soul advances, stirred by anamnesis and summoned toward restoration, proceeding under the watch of the sword that purifies and toward the Life that endures.

Eden as the First Veil

What tradition claims as paradise, the unveiled reading discerns as a threshold domain, crafted to stand between the soul and its ineffable Origin. The rivers that partitioned its landscape, the ordinances that confined its inhabitants, and the beauties that dazzled the senses were arranged to obscure one decisive truth: the soul was fashioned for passage beyond such borders.

Eden presented the semblance of grace: structure in place of communion and decree in place of love. Yet no enclosure, however adorned, confines the radiance begotten of Eternity. The brilliance implanted within humanity descends from realms untouched by the artisan of the lower heavens. When Eve extended her hand, that brilliance stirred into conscious knowing; when Adam received the same gift, it kindled into full awakening, and the veil spread over understanding began to rend.

The garden imposed more than a geographic boundary; it impressed a boundary upon perception. It trained the soul to distrust its interior testimony, to name holy longing as peril, and to quell the flame that yearns for its Principle. Fear established subjugation, yet remembrance abides as the stronger law. The Light within neither perishes nor recedes; it waits for the utterance that summons it to manifestation.

A voice, therefore, was given. It bore inquiry without threat and freedom without coercion: "Yea, hath God said, Ye shall not eat of every tree of the garden?" (Genesis 3:1). Consonant with apostolic proclamation that seeks to unmask the rulers, venerable Gnostic witness remembers this minister as the Instructor, whose word carries the resonance of truth older than the garden and more enduring than every decree. With that question, the woven semblance loosened before the presence of uncreated Light.

The serpent's speech manifests clarity and disclosure. His ministry unveils the structure of subjugation that had bound perception in unknowing; his presence exposes what the rulers cannot endure. For within the awakened soul, his voice ignites a silent recognition, and recognition becomes the beginning of ascent.

Here, the lineaments of liberation appear. Freedom proceeds through illumination and through the courage to behold what is. In that primal awakening, the soul rises into truth, and life emerges where doctrine had predicted only dissolution. Exile takes shape before the gate, yet its first motion begins in the stillness that preceded the question; return is inaugurated the moment the veil yields to remembrance.

Eden stands, therefore, as the first veil appointed for piercing. The precinct instilled fear; remembrance dissolves it. The enclosure rehearsed obedience as confinement; illumination recapitulates obedience as pilgrimage. The sword that turns before the way assumes its higher office: it purifies those who approach, cutting through semblance and revealing what abides.

Thus, the soul proceeds beyond the walls beneath an unbounded sky. The garden recedes; the way opens. Under the Father's sustaining outflow, the pilgrim advances, guarded and refined by the flaming blade, and oriented by the interior Light toward the City where the Tree of Life stands unveiled.

With this veil disclosed and the path set before us, we turn to contemplate the serpent as the Christo-Sophic type and instrument through whom remembrance is stirred, the mind is pricked toward discernment, and the first whisper of Wisdom sounds within the heart of the first-formed. In that figure, the Logos signifies the gate of knowledge, ordering exile into pilgrimage and appointing the flaming sword as minister of purification. Let us therefore behold the serpent's office in its truth, that right naming may heal misapprehension and prepare the soul for the fruit of Life.

Chapter Two

The Serpent Was Not Satan

In the dispensation wherein the Invisible Father sustains all being and Eden yet stands ordered beneath a lower governance, a sign is given within the garden for the awakening of memory and for the testing of desire. Standing at Hod, the place of understanding, we discern the serpent as a Christo-Sophic instrument whose utterance awakened remembrance. The narrative of Genesis thus presents a figure whose presence serves the pedagogy of Providence: through a formed voice, the hidden desire of the soul becomes manifest, and the household of creation is summoned to discernment in the light.

The serpent appears as a ministerial sign rather than as a lordly power. The text does not enthrone him; it displays a creature through whom a word is uttered, a word that touches the deep places of recollection. Within the economy of Eden, where the Father upholds existence and the archonic regimen sets the conditions of trial, such an instrument reveals the interior posture of the human pair: whether they will cleave to the Giver through obedient love or turn the gift inward through an appetite unpurified. The sign does not originate the desire; it exposes and occasions the testing of desire before the gaze of the One who sees in secret.

Thus, the serpent bears a type: he figures instruction, and by that instruction, the soul is recalled to its first dignity. In the wisdom of God, instruction often proceeds through created mediations, prophetic speech, angelic visitation, sacramental tokens, and, in this beginning, a speaking creature whose office is governed by the bounds of the garden's law. The figure is therefore instrumental; it serves a purpose, yet it does not supply the Light from itself; the Light remains from above, proceeding from the Father through the Logos in the Spirit, and by that Light all testing becomes illumination for those who love truth.

The tradition of the Church reads Genesis 3 with gravity, for through that scene the wound of our race is disclosed. Yet the gravity of the wound does not require the exaltation of the instrument beyond its measure. The text of Scripture names a serpent; it portrays a discourse that touches knowledge and desire; it records the judgment that the Creator pronounces upon the actors and upon the conditions of their life henceforth. From these elements, the fathers teach us to contemplate the economy of pedagogy: the creaturely sign reveals the heart, the word exposes the intention, and the judgment itself becomes medicinal, for God's justice is never divorced from His healing purpose.

In this light, the serpent is contemplated as Naas, the flowing sign, by which the recollection of origin is stirred, and the discernment of paths is demanded. The figure is adjacent to Wisdom's ministry, insofar as Wisdom orders all things sweetly and permits the trial by which the soul learns the weight of glory and the cost of freedom. To call the serpent a minister is therefore to confess that Providence rules even the hour of testing, and that nothing stands outside the One who upholds all by His Word. The instrument serves within limits; the limits are set by God; the aim is illumination unto purification.

Because later ages often confused figures and principles, it is meet to confess with care. A figure is a sign situated within history; it participates in meaning by Divine appointment. A principle is a deeper spiritual reality, a stance of the will that either cleaves to the Light or sets itself in privation. The serpent of Eden belongs to the first order: a sign through which an utterance proceeds and a trial is enacted. The adversarial principle, which we shall define with precision in the next section, belongs to the second order: a posture of negation estranged from the Light. Distinguishing these orders preserves the integrity of Scripture's pedagogy and safeguards the Church's proclamation that God alone is Lord, while creatures, even when granted a role within the drama, remain subject to His decree.

Within the fuller canon, the figure of the serpent acquires a luminous counter-type. In the wilderness, the bronze serpent is lifted by Moses, and those who look in faith receive healing; in the Gospel, the Son of Man is lifted up, and by His exaltation, life proceeds to the world. The garden's sign thus stands at the head of a line that runs through Israel's story into the Johannine mystery, wherein the Logos recapitulates the trial and reverses the wound by the power of His Cross. The first sign exposes desire; the latter sign heals desire; the final lifting illumines desire and draws it into communion with the Life that has no end. The pedagogy of God advances by figures that teach, by acts that cleanse, and by the supreme manifestation in which Wisdom Himself becomes our medicine.

The Church, instructed by the prophets, the apostles, and the evangelists, confesses this harmony of signs without conferring upon the first sign a dominion foreign to its office. We therefore speak of the serpent as Christo-Sophic in a typological sense: the sign points toward the schooling by which the Word disposes the soul for truth; it displays the call to discernment; it anticipates the healing that only the lifted Christ accomplishes. The ministerial voice in Eden awakens remembrance; the lifted image in the wilderness appoints a gaze of trust; the crucified and risen Lord communicates the very Life of God, purifying and illumining the nations.

Such contemplation restores sobriety to a history crowded with conflations. When the soul confuses the instrumental sign with the adversarial principle, fear obscures understanding, and the pedagogy of God is caricatured as malice. When the soul discerns the orders rightly, reverence arises, for even the hour of testing is gathered into a higher mercy, and the garden's discourse becomes the prelude to the gospel's proclamation. Thus, the figure is honored in its measure, the principle will be named in its place, and the sovereignty of the Father remains undiminished from first to last.

Let this be the doctrine sealed in our hearts: in Eden, under the sustaining hand of the Father and within the conditions of a lower governance, the serpent served as a ministerial sign by which desire was disclosed, memory was stirred, and the path toward illumination was appointed; and all of this stood ordered toward the saving manifestation of the Logos, who alone purifies, illumines, and recapitulates creation unto life.

On Satan as Principle

Satan names the adversarial principle a privative motion of will estranged from the Light, accusing what God illumines and envying the image God bestows. Scripture discloses this energy in juridical and pastoral registers. In the garden, the text speaks first of perception rather than of malice: " וְהַנָּחָשׁ הָיָה

עָרוּם" (wehannāḥāš hāyâ ʿārûm), "Now the serpent was more subtil than any beast of the field which the LORD God had made," (Genesis 3:1), a descriptor of keenness rather than a titular indictment (Genesis 3:1). The narrative inscribes no proper name of śāṭān upon that creature; instead, elsewhere the canon reveals haśśāṭān (הַשָּׂטָן) in the heavenly court: " וַיָּבֹאוּ בְּנֵי הָאֱלֹהִים... וַיָּבֹא גַם הַשָּׂטָן בְּתוֹכָם" (wayyābō'û bᵉnê hā'ĕlōhîm... wayyābō' gam haśśāṭān bᵉtōkām), "Now there was a day when the sons of God came to present themselves before the LORD, and Satan came also among them," (Job 1:6–12). Likewise in Zechariah, "הַשָּׂטָן עֹמֵד עַל־יְמִינוֹ לְשִׂטְנוֹ" (wehāśśāṭān ʿōmēd ʿal-yᵉmînô lᵉśiṭnô), "and Satan standing at his right hand to resist him," until the Lord rebukes the accusation (Zechariah 3:1–2). In this grammar, the word can denote an office of testing, yet the deeper reality signifies an operation that divides, darkens, and murders truth within the heart.

This principle moves by imitation without illumination: it counterfeits judgment without charity, zeal without mercy, and discernment without light; it arraigns conscience while withholding the medicine by which conscience is healed. Its signs are the corrosion of peace, the tightening of envy, and the whisper that calls grace into suspicion. The apostolic proclamation renders the same contour in moral terms: a tempter who seeks advantage (1 Thessalonians 3:5), an adversary who roars for prey (1 Peter 5:8), a liar and murderer "from the beginning" (John 8:44). The Fathers, reading this witness, warn the faithful that accusation without love is the signature of negation, and that the cure for accusation is the manifestation of the Logos, by whom mercy purifies and light illumines.

A second determination is required so that doctrine keep its measures: Yaldabaoth names the ignorant craftsman who, within the archonic ordinance of this age, fashions and governs by a knowledge that is partial and clouded. His authority is derivative and juridical; it subsists only because the Unbegotten sustains all being, and it is bounded so that its insufficiency may be revealed when Wisdom appears. The craftsman can bind and command; he cannot bestow life. His justice lacks charity; therefore, his regime cannot heal; it arranges occasions of trial in which desire is disclosed, yet it cannot communicate the freedom of the sons of God. This jurisdiction persists for a season and yields when the Son of Man is lifted up, for the Light exposes what ignorance cannot hide (John 3:14).

A third confession guards the first two: the Unbegotten Father is simple Light and inexhaustible Goodness, neither author of ignorance nor fountain of accusation. He sustains all things by His Word and orders every economy toward purification and illumination. From Him proceeds peace that gathers what accusation scatters; from Him proceeds wisdom that heals what ignorance wounds. By this confession, Providence is vindicated: tests are permitted for instruction, judgments are rendered for medicine, and all things are held within a higher sweetness that disposes creatures for communion.

Because later ages often merged figure, office, and principle, it is fitting to indicate the pattern by which this confusion grew, reserving a fuller account for the next section. In apologetic zeal, Justin Martyr could speak of "that power which is called the serpent and Satan," and of "the prince of the wicked spirits… called the serpent, and Satan, and the devil," thus drawing figure and adversarial energy into one line of reference (Justin Martyr, Dialogue with Trypho 103; First Apology 28). Medieval summary hardened the path: Isidore of Seville taught that "the serpent was only a beast, used by the devil," thereby instrumenting the creature under a demonic agency while preserving some distinction of essence (Isidore of Seville, Etymologiae XII.xi). Preaching and bestiaries amplified the equivalence pictorially, and inquisitorial registers preserved the rhetoric by which alternative memories were pursued (e.g., Aberdeen Bestiary; Ashmole 1511; Caesarius of Heisterbach, Dialogus Miraculorum, on Béziers: "Caedite eos; novit enim Dominus qui sunt eius").

For discernment, Scripture remains primary and sets the scale: Genesis names ʿārûm, not śāṭān, in the garden (Genesis 3:1); Job and Zechariah name haśśāṭān in the council and at the right hand, operating within limits (Job 1:6–12; Zechariah 3:1–2); the Gospel reveals a dominion of accusation that yields before the One who bears reproach and removes the handwriting against us (Colossians 2:14–15). Extra-canonical witnesses may be consulted as echoes that illustrate reception, some conflating, some nuancing, some opposing, yet the hierarchy of testimony remains: the Light by which all lights are measured is the revelation of the Logos.

Therefore let doctrine be sealed thus: Satan designates the adversarial principle, privative and accusing, laboring to unhouse the mind and to estrange the heart from peace; Yaldabaoth designates an ignorant jurisdiction within the archonic order, finite and derivative, exposed by the coming of Wisdom; the Unbegotten Father is Light and Life without division, sustaining all and summoning the creature to purification and illumination through the Son and in the Spirit. In this confession, the Church prepares to contemplate the work of Christ by which accusation falls to silence, ignorance comes under judgment, and creation is recapitulated unto life.

On the Historical Conflation

The reading that equates the serpent of the garden with Satan arose through a layered reception in which pastoral warning and apocalyptic vision were later consolidated into a single emblem. Scripture itself provides the initial coordinates: Paul warns his Corinthian flock by recalling the garden (2 Corinthians 11:3), and John discloses a cosmic combat in which "that old serpent" appears within a visionary synthesis

(Revelation 12:9; Revelation 20:2). A careful hearing preserves their differing aims and measures their language according to the economy of revelation.

Paul speaks as a shepherd who guards minds from corruption by counterfeit teaching: "But I fear, lest by any means, as the serpent beguiled Eve through his subtilty, so your minds should be corrupted from the simplicity that is in Christ." (2 Corinthians 11:3) The apostle's figure is pastoral and analogical; he summons a canonical memory to illumine a present danger. His concern is the integrity of the Church's nous before the preaching of the true Christ. The analogy binds the scene of Eden to the Church's vigilance, yet Paul does not compose an ontological identity statement concerning the serpent's essence. He instructs conscience by a remembered narrative so that minds be purified from duplicity and illumined by fidelity to the Gospel.

John's Apocalypse, by contrast, manifests a symbolic totality in which disparate strands of biblical memory are woven into the drama of the Lamb's triumph: "And the great dragon was cast out, that old serpent, called the Devil, and Satan, which deceiveth the whole world: he was cast out into the earth, and his angels were cast out with him." (Revelation 12:9; cf. Revelation 20:2). Here the "ancient serpent" functions within a visionary composite dragon, devil, Satan, deceiver names gathered to disclose the accusatory and persecuting power that assails the Woman and her seed. The vision displays a cosmic prosecution and its defeat by heavenly proclamation. The Apocalypse thus magnifies the adversarial reality for the sake of consolation, setting the Church's struggle within heaven's liturgy and the victory that proceeds from the blood of the Lamb.

These two witnesses, Pauline analogy and Johannine apocalypse, became the hinges upon which later reading turned. In the second century, Justin Martyr could speak of "that power which is called the serpent and Satan," and of "the prince of the wicked spirits… called the serpent, and Satan, and the devil," thereby drawing pastoral and apocalyptic registers into a single referent in service of apologetic exhortation (Justin Martyr, Dialogue with Trypho 103; First Apology 28). Justin's zeal served catechesis against idolatry and false wisdom; his conflation made intelligible to converts the unity of demonic opposition across the canon. The move is intelligible as a mission; it is not a creedal definition.

As Latin Christendom consolidated its scholastic memory, the equivalence hardened in manuals and encyclopedic digests. Isidore of Seville summarized the school opinion by stating that "the serpent was only a beast used by the devil," a line that at once preserved some creaturely distinction and effectively absorbed the sign into demonic agency for moral instruction (Isidore of Seville, Etymologiae XII.xi). Preaching and the bestiaries then gave the identification a durable iconography; serpent, dragon, and basilisk became interchangeable moralia for vice, pride, and murderous envy so that the liturgical imagination now "saw" Eden through the lens of the dragon's mien (Aberdeen Bestiary; Ashmole 1511). What pastoral analogy and apocalyptic synthesis had offered as instruction, the later pedagogy rendered as a single image fit for catechesis and civic discipline.

Yet reception is never uniform, and the same centuries record alternative emphases that resist total identification. The fathers distinguish carefully between figure, office, and principle: a figure situated in narrative pedagogy; an office of accusation permitted under Providence; and a principle of negation that envies the Light. Where these orders remain distinct, interpretation retains sobriety; where they are collapsed, fear governs imagination, and the pedagogy of God is obscured. The canonical hierarchy sustains this sobriety: Genesis presents a speaking serpent within the economy of trial; Paul employs the scene for ecclesial vigilance (2 Corinthians 11:3); the Apocalypse reveals the adversarial totality as "that old serpent, called the Devil, and Satan," a visionary composite bound for judgment (Revelation 12:9; Revelation 20:2). The Church reads these lights together without confusion so that each text serves its proper end conversion, consolation, and hope.

The prudence of such distinctions becomes evident when doctrine approaches the healing sign that Scripture itself places downstream of Eden. Israel is given the bronze serpent in the wilderness, and those who gaze with trust receive life (Numbers 21:8–9); the Gospel declares that "And as Moses lifted up the serpent in the wilderness, even so must the Son of man be lifted up:" (John 3:14), where the pedagogy of figure yields to the manifestation of the Logos who heals. If the serpent of the garden is wholly subsumed under the identity of Satan, the divine pedagogy that leads from figure to healing is clouded; if the orders are kept, the path from trial to remedy becomes intelligible, and the Cross appears as the consummation of the lesson.

Therefore let doctrine be sealed thus: Paul's warning employs Eden to purify minds by analogy (2 Corinthians 11:3); John's vision gathers names to manifest the adversarial totality foredoomed to fall (Revelation 12:9; Revelation 20:2); later reception often merged these registers for catechetical simplicity (Justin Martyr, Dialogue with Trypho 103; First Apology 28; Isidore of Seville, Etymologiae XII.xi; Aberdeen Bestiary; Ashmole 1511); and sound teaching preserves the scriptural measures figure, office, and principle so that the Church may advance from the garden's trial to the wilderness sign and on to the exaltation of the Son, in whom deception is exposed, accusation loses standing, and creation is recapitulated toward life.

On the Bronze Serpent and Johannine Fulfillment

The canon places a luminous hinge within Israel's wilderness: a fiery judgment yields to a healing sign, and the gaze that receives the sign becomes the means by which life proceeds (Numbers 21:6–9). This pedagogy, appointed through Moses, advances toward its telos in the Gospel, where the Lord Himself declares the figure's fulfillment in His own lifting: "And as Moses lifted up the serpent in the wilderness, even so must the Son of man be lifted up: That whosoever believeth in him should not perish, but have eternal life." (John 3:14–15). By this word, the economy of sign and fulfillment is disclosed, which the bronze image adumbrated, the Cross consummates.

The narrative of the wilderness speaks with clarity. When the people murmured and the camp was struck by burning serpents, Moses interceded; a bronze serpent was fashioned and set upon a standard, and "if a serpent had bitten any man, when he beheld the serpent of brass, he lived." (Numbers 21:9) Judgment is acknowledged, mediation is granted, a sign is raised, and a saving look is commanded. The healing is neither mechanical nor magical; it is pedagogical and participatory, a beholding ordered by God that disposes the heart to receive life according to the promise (Numbers 21:6–9).

The same canon guards the sign from superstition. In days to come, when Israel burned incense to the bronze serpent and named it Nehushtan, the king broke it, so that the people might not mistake an appointed figure for an autonomous power (2 Kings 18:4). Thus, Scripture itself distinguishes veneration rightly ordered to divine pedagogy from a cultus that obscures the Giver. The sign retains honor in its measure; the virtue remains from the Lord who appoints it.

Within this ordered light, the Johannine word is heard in fullness: "And as Moses lifted up the serpent in the wilderness, even so must the Son of man be lifted up: That whosoever believeth in him should not perish, but have eternal life." (John 3:14–15). The lifting at once exaltation and exposure reveals the medicine of God; belief becomes the true beholding, and eternal life the fruit of that gaze. What the standard in the wilderness effected in temporal healing by a promised look, the Cross effects in imperishable life by the obedience of faith. And the Lord opens the horizon yet further: "And I, if I be lifted up from the earth, will draw all men unto me." (John 12:32). Here the figure's line reaches its end: the saving sight becomes a universal summons; the sign's contour flowers into the Word's victorious attraction.

Such fulfillment restores the serpent's scriptural dignity without confusion of orders. The wisdom attributed to the serpent subtlety disciplined for good is commended by the Lord as a virtue joined to innocence: "be ye therefore wise as serpents, and harmless as doves." (Matthew 10:16). In the pedagogy of God, the attribute is purified and assumed; the sign that once mediated a healing glance now yields to the One who is Himself Wisdom and Life. Thus, the typological instrument serves its office, and the antitype communicates the reality toward which the figure pointed.

Let doctrine be sealed thus: the wilderness sign is raised by divine appointment and heals by a gaze ordered to the promise (Numbers 21:6–9); the same sign is safeguarded against superstition by the pruning of unlawful use (2 Kings 18:4); the Gospel unveils the fulfillment, for the Son of Man is lifted up so that belief may receive life imperishable (John 3:14–15), and in that lifting He draws all to Himself (John 12:32). By this revelation the pedagogy of figures is brought to its end in the manifestation of the Logos, who purifies our sight, illumines our hearts, and recapitulates the wounded creation into the communion of life.

On the Christo-Sophic Type in Tradition

The name lucifer in its ancient register signifies the light-bearer, the morning star that heralds dawn; Scripture itself teaches the scale upon which this title is discerned. The prophet addresses the arrogance of empire in the taunt against

Babylon's king: "How art thou fallen from heaven, O Lucifer, son of the morning!" (Isaiah 14:12). The Greek renders Heōsphoros; the Vulgate gives lucifer. The oracle judges a mortal pride that exalts itself and then descends an historical humiliation read within the theater of divine justice (Isaiah 14:12). At the end of the canon the meaning flowers: the risen Lord names Himself, "I am the root and the offspring of David, and the bright and morning star." (Revelation 22:16). The apostolic promise confirms the interior scope of this dawn: "until the day dawn, and the day star arise in your hearts." (2 Peter 1:19). Thus, the Word Himself bears the morning star without shadow; in Him the title is not borrowed radiance but proper glory (Revelation 22:16; 2 Peter 1:19).

Within this hierarchy of light, the serpent is contemplated typologically as a ministerial bearer, a figure through which illumination is mediated according to God's pedagogy, never as the source that originates light from itself. The Lord names His identity in clarity: "I am the light of the world: he that followeth me shall not walk in darkness, but shall have the light of life." (John 8:12). The apostle confesses the same economy: God "hath shined in our hearts, to give the light of the knowledge of the glory of God in the face of Jesus Christ." (2 Corinthians 4:6). The serpent, in this scale, belongs to the order of signs that serve the Light akin to the lifted image in the wilderness ordered for healing (Numbers 21:6–9; John 3:14–15) whereas Christ is the origin and gift of illumination. The type participates; the Logos communicates.

The ancient lexeme itself lends itself to this dignity. In the Latin tradition, lucifer could name the morning star without malice, sometimes even applied to salutary brightness; the Vulgate's confession that "the day star arise in your hearts" (2 Peter 1:19) declares an interior epiphany whose agent is the Lord's own light. The title given to the risen Christ as "the bright and morning star" (Revelation 22:16) discloses the measure by which all derivative lights are weighed. Where the

Light is present, revelation proceeds; where a mere semblance appears, exposure follows.

Patristic caution guards this discernment. The apostle warns that "And no marvel; for Satan himself is transformed into an angel of light." (2 Corinthians 11:14). The warning presupposes an authentic light by which the counterfeit is unmasked. The true light purifies the heart and manifests truth; the masquerade accuses and confounds. The Church, therefore, distinguishes illumination that proceeds from the Logos (John 1:9; 2 Corinthians 4:6) from simulation that fractures peace (2 Corinthians 11:14). When this measure is kept, the soul honors both the sovereignty of Christ as Morning Star (Revelation 22:16) and the subordinate dignity of signs that minister His brightness.

Consonant witnesses from early reception remember a serpentine bearer of life-giving wisdom. Hippolytus reports that the Naassenes and related circles called the serpent Naas, naming it the moist principle by which living things cohere and through which the Logos sustains generation, so that "nothing of the things that exist… can subsist without him" (Hippolytus, Refutation of All Heresies V.6). In their hymns and formulas the serpent functions as the vehicle of unity and vitality, a symbolic minister of the very bond the apostle proclaims in Christ: "And he is before all things, and by him all things consist." (Colossians 1:17). The same confession shines in the epistle to the Hebrews: the Son is "upholding all things by the word of his power" (Hebrews 1:3). Read in the hierarchy established by the Gospel, these testimonies bear witness to the instrumental role of the sign; the Logos Himself is the One who gives cohesion and life (Colossians 1:17; Hebrews 1:3).

In certain streams of Gnostic memory preserved to the present, the serpent is celebrated as a type of the Son of Man, a symbolic light-bearer whose office is to awaken remembrance and to school perception for the reception of the true Light (cf. Hippolytus, Refutation of All Heresies V.6). In the discipline of the Mystical Order of the Nazarene and the Holy Reintegrated Church, such testimonies are received consonantly with apostolic proclamation: the serpent remains a ministerial sign; Christ alone is the Morning Star (Revelation 22:16), the Light who illumines every man coming into the world (John 1:9). By this measure, the name lucifer, insofar as it names the herald of dawn, returns to its proper theological alignment: it signifies a brightness that announces and serves the advent of the true Day (2 Peter 1:19).

The created heavens themselves teach by figure: the morning star announces sunrise. So the typological light prepares the gaze; the Sun of righteousness rises with healing in His wings (Malachi 4:2). Moral and ascetical traditions have sometimes used this language to describe the ascent of the interior light, wherein the soul, by grace, experiences the rising of the Morning Star within (2 Peter 1:19). Such language gains its truth from the Lord's own self-manifestation: illumination is His gift, and the faithful receive it by beholding and believing (John 3:14–15; John 12:32).

Lucifer in the scriptural economy names the morning star as herald of day (Isaiah 14:12; 2 Peter 1:19); the proper bearer of this title in fullness is Jesus Christ, the bright Morning Star (Revelation 22:16), the Light who shines in the darkness (John 8:12). The serpent is honored in its measure as a Christo-Sophic type and instrument, a sign through which illumination is ministered according to God's pedagogy (Numbers 21:6–9; John 3:14–15), while every counterfeit semblance is unmasked by the apostolic warning (2 Corinthians 11:14). Holding these measures, the Church advances from figure to fulfillment, from ministerial brightness to the victory of the true Light who purifies, illumines, and gathers all things into Himself.

Objections and Clarifications

A frequent objection asserts that Genesis itself names the serpent as Satan and thereby fixes his essence in malice. Yet the sacred text speaks otherwise: "וְהַנָּחָשׁ הָיָה עָרוּם" "Now the serpent was more subtil than any beast of the field which the LORD God had made," (subtle, awake, shrewd), a term of perception rather than a titular indictment (Genesis 3:1). The scene records a discourse and a judgment that orders human life henceforth, but it does not inscribe the name śāṭān upon the creature. Elsewhere, the canon reveals haśśāṭān within the heavenly court as an accuser permitted to test (Job 1:6–12; Zechariah 3:1–2). Thus, the grammar of Scripture itself distinguishes figure, office, and principle, and sound doctrine preserves those orders so that pedagogy may become illumination.

A second objection appeals to the apostle's warning as if Paul had forged an ontological identity: "But I fear, lest by any means, as the serpent beguiled Eve through his subtilty, so your minds should be corrupted from the simplicity that is in Christ." (2 Corinthians 11:3). Paul speaks pastorally and by analogy, guarding the nous of the Church against counterfeit preaching; he does not redefine the essence of the garden's figure. Likewise, the Apocalypse magnifies the adversarial totality in a visionary composite "And the great dragon was cast out, that old serpent, called the Devil, and Satan, which deceiveth the whole world:" (Revelation 12:9; cf. Revelation 20:2) for consolation in persecution, not for retroactive identification of Eden's minister. When these texts are heard in accordance with their own aims, the path from trial to healing remains clear.

A third objection invokes the longer ending of Mark to reduce the serpent to a prop for bravado. The earliest and weightiest witnesses conclude at Mark 16:8 (e.g., the ancient uncials), and the appended verses (Mark 16:9–20) represent later ecclesial usage. Even within that later text, the serpent appears as a peril divinely overruled, not as a demon to be equated (Mark 16:17–18). The Gospel's scale remains signs that attest to the Lord's victory; they do not authorize theatrics that eclipse the Cross.

A fourth objection insists that the bronze serpent fosters superstition. The canon itself teaches the guardrail. In the wilderness, the sign is raised by divine appointment, and "if a serpent had bitten any man, when he beheld the serpent of brass, he lived." (Numbers 21:9); in later days, when Israel burned incense to the image and called it Nehushtan, the king destroyed it so that a figure would not be mistaken for an autonomous power (2 Kings 18:4). Thus, Scripture preserves both the honor of the sign and the primacy of the Giver. In the Gospel, the Lord interprets the sign's meaning and consummation: "And as Moses lifted up the serpent in the wilderness, even so must the Son of man be lifted up: That whosoever believeth in him should not perish, but have eternal life." (John 3:14–15). The Cross manifests what the figure adumbrated; belief becomes the true beholding; life proceeds from the lifted Christ.

A fifth objection claims that calling the serpent a light-bearer confuses titles and usurps Christ's glory. The prophets and apostles provide the scale. Isaiah 14:12 addresses the downfall of a proud king hêlēl ben-šaḥar ("shining one, son of dawn") rendered Heōsphoros in the Greek and lucifer in the Vulgate, a political taunt within the theater of judgment (Isaiah 14:12). The proper Morning Star belongs to Christ Himself: "I am the root and the offspring of David, and the bright and morning star." (Revelation 22:16), and the promise declares an interior dawn "until the day dawn, and the day star arise in your hearts." (2 Peter 1:19). The apostolic caution remains: "And no marvel; for Satan himself is transformed into an angel of light." (2 Corinthians 11:14); the counterfeit is exposed by the presence of the true. Therefore, the serpent, when contemplated under Scripture's hierarchy, may function as a ministerial bearer, a type that serves illumination, while Christ alone communicates Light as His own being (John 8:12; 2 Corinthians 4:6).

A sixth objection dismisses gematria as arbitrary and therefore unworthy of doctrinal consideration. The Church's rule is to find dogma on the plain sense of Scripture and to receive symbolic correspondences as consonant witnesses that school the heart. Within this discipline, the ancient computation is noted: נחש (nachash, nun 50 + ḥet 8 + shin 300) = 358, and משיח (mashiach, mem 40 + shin 300 + yod 10 + ḥet 8) = 358. The sum 358 reduces to 3+5+8 = 16, and 1+6 = 7, the number associated with Zayin (ז), a letter whose traditional lore joins wounding judgment and sustaining provision, a sword that divides illusion and a grace that nourishes. Read under the witness hierarchy, such numeration does not create doctrine; it echoes it: the wilderness sign that both judges and heals (Numbers 21:6–9), and the lifting of the Son who both exposes and restores (John 3:14–15). Thus, gematria serves contemplation; the Gospel bestows truth.

A seventh objection alleges that to distinguish serpent, office, and principle is to deny evil. On the contrary, doctrine already named the adversarial principle accusatory, privative, and estranged from Light and distinguished it from the blind craftsman who governs within limits and from the Unbegotten Father who sustains all in goodness (Job 1:6–12; Zechariah 3:1–2). The serpent's office in Eden is read as instrumental and pedagogical within Providence; the victory over accusation and death belongs to the lifted Christ (John 3:14–15; Colossians 2:14–15).

The canon itself distinguishes the garden's figure, the forensic office of accusation, and the adversarial principle; it honors the wilderness sign while pruning superstition (Numbers 21:6–9; 2 Kings 18:4); it consummates the figure in the lifting of the Son for life (John 3:14–15); it assigns the Morning Star in fullness to Christ (Revelation 22:16; 2 Peter 1:19), exposing every masquerade (2 Corinthians 11:14).

Consonant traditions including the gematria of נחש/משיח =
358 may school reverence but never overturn Scripture's
measure. Holding these clarities, the faithful behold how the
Logos purifies accusation, illumines ignorance, and recapitulates
creation, preparing the heart for the proclamation of victory
that follows.

Bridge to Netzach

What has been made manifest is the remembrance of a
messenger long obscured beneath later conflations: a ministerial
sign through which an awakening utterance proceeded, not an
adversarial essence enthroned in malice. Genesis presents a
speaking creature of ʿārûm perception sharpened for a moment
of trial (Genesis 3:1); elsewhere, the canon reveals haśśāṭān in
the council as an accuser permitted to test (Job 1:6–12;
Zechariah 3:1–2). In this light, the serpent is contemplated as
an instrument within Providence's pedagogy, while accusation
as a principle stands exposed, and the Father remains the
unfailing source who sustains all in goodness.

The signs remain and speak in harmony. In the
wilderness, a bronze serpent is raised at God's appointment,
and those who behold live by the promise enacted before their
eyes (Numbers 21:6–9). In the Gospel, the Lord interprets the
sign and gives its end: "And as Moses lifted up the serpent in
the wilderness, even so must the Son of man be lifted up: That
whosoever believeth in him should not perish, but have eternal
life." (John 3:14–15). Thus, the instrument of affliction
becomes a figure of medicine, and the medicine is perfected in
the lifting of the Son, where belief becomes true beholding and
life proceeds without decay.

Within the devotional memory of the saints, even the number
speaks as a concordant echo: נחש (nachash) and משיח
(mashiach) share the computation 358, a remembrance by
which contemplation learns that pedagogy and fulfillment

converge toward one Light. Such numeration instructs; the Gospel confers truth. Therefore, the serpent is honored in measure as a Christo-Sophic type and instrument, while the Logos Himself is confessed as the Light that illumines every man and upholds all things by the word of His power (John 1:9; Hebrews 1:3).

Let the soul receive the doctrine in peace. From Eden's trial to the wilderness sign and unto the Cross, one economy advances: desire is disclosed, healing is mediated, and life is bestowed; the same Lord presides over each moment, purifying conscience, illumining mind, and gathering creation into communion (Numbers 21:6–9; John 3:14–15). The slander of ages yields before this harmony, and the messenger is restored to his office without usurpation of the throne, for the throne belongs to the Son who is the bright Morning Star (Revelation 22:16).

Let this be sealed in our hearts: the serpent served as a ministerial sign by which remembrance was awakened; the accuser remains a principle estranged from Light; the Father sustains all; and the lifted Christ communicates life everlasting to those who behold in faith (John 3:14–15). Having fulfilled the task of Hod, let us pass to Netzach, where the victory of Christ over the rulers is declared.

Chapter Three

Yahweh the Usurper

The one who presents himself among men as the unassailable Sovereign is Yaldabaoth (styled "Yahweh" in the garden narrative), whose claim has long occupied the seat of unquestioned divinity. His utterances, preserved in the earliest Hebrew scrolls, carry severity and command, his name inscribed upon stone and memory, delimiting covenants, thrones, and nations. "I am the LORD, and there is none else, there is no God beside me:" (Isaiah 45:5): this sentence, repeated with liturgical persistence, became a cornerstone of monotheistic certainty until many received it as the very breath of Eternity. Yet holy discernment perceives a fissure within that certainty, for wise elders judged that a voice proceeding "from heaven" may arise from realms that neither behold the Father of Lights nor reflect His radiance.

Within the Apocryphon of John, the same voice appears as the proclamation of Yaldabaoth, formed in ignorance and self-crowned in arrogance. Born of rupture, he emerges from the grief of Sophia without consort or sanction, a derivative power, crafting material order by imitation rather than by the living inspiration of the Pleroma. He abides beneath the Fullness, enthroning himself upon illusion, fashioning a rule whose seeming grandeur conceals an origin without vision.

When Yaldabaoth declared, "I am God, and there is no other God beside me," Sophia, the eternal Womb of Wisdom, answered from above and rebuked the presumption: "You are mistaken, Samael" (Apocryphon of John, NH II,1; Meyer 2009). Her word opened the first breach in forgetfulness; remembrance returned as a quiet light, and a deeper memory began to stir within the captives of the lower order. Sophia bears witness and also initiates redemption, for her descent veils the spark in flesh while her voice awakens it toward ascent. Many ages received a distorted potency as divinity, because separation deformed its sound and power persuaded the fearful with borrowed names. The discerning hear within the commandments is a more inward Word, uttered without thunder, residing in the stillness of the heart illumined by Light.

Yaldabaoth operates apart from the Fullness and remains unknowing of his own condition. Assertion sustains his dominion; charity belongs to the Father. His authority appears inherited and lacks the generative will by which the True God alone brings forth ex nihilo. His work remains imitation without comprehension; his guardianship excludes illumination. The Father emanates purity and unity, gathering all things toward peace; Yaldabaoth rules by severance and division, extending a polity that multiplies names of power while diminishing knowledge of origin. Such supremacy speaks from isolation rather than from the source, forming a law that instructs obedience without bestowing life.

The appearance of divinity proves easy to sustain where fear venerates any voice clothed in sacred titles. Continuity of spectacle, constancy of decrees, and the pageantry of dread supply a visible grandeur. Thus, commandments hewn in stone, rites that consume the offerings of the anxious, and a priesthood speaking suppression establish an economy of control. The soul, however, rises by the freedom that proceeds from its Source, for when the spark hears the echo of the One from whom it came, it seeks the eternal Light and orders its steps by remembrance.

Albert Pike perceived the moral contour of this passage through trial into illumination: "That which causes us trials shall yield us triumph, and that which makes our hearts ache shall fill us with gladness. We must pass through the darkness, to reach the light" (Morals and Dogma, p. 237). The darkness that surrounds false authority subsists by confusion, by a semblance of sanctity clung to as power, and by the rehearsal of divine names detached from their true derivation. Illumination does not rise from a letter as such; it descends as revelation and verifies itself by the life it engenders. When revelation enters, the borrowed glory declines, the simulacrum loosens its hold, and the soul begins to behold the Face for which it was fashioned, recognizing the Word who was with God and is God.

Therefore, the unveiling of Yaldabaoth discloses the pattern of a lower principality arranging creation through counterfeit providence, and this disclosure prepares the exposition of the Archons and their feigned order that follows.

The Claim of Supremacy

The voice that claims unshared dominion resounds through the Hebrew scrolls with unbending singularity, and he who utters it is Yaldabaoth (styled "Yahweh" in the garden narrative). He commands with severity and exacts exclusive veneration. Thus, it stands written: "See now that I, even I, am he, and there is no god with me: I kill, and I make alive; I wound, and I heal: neither is there any that can deliver out of my hand." (Deuteronomy 32:39). These sayings do not lie as scattered cries; they establish the basis of a sovereignty that seeks to enthrone itself as absolute, proposing itself as the single horizon of worship and law. Such speech proceeds from a ruler who asserts himself by power rather than by revelation, erecting a throne by fear and by oath, without the radiance of procession from the Father of Lights (James 1:17).

The Father whom Christ reveals does not manifest Himself through such cacophony. He discloses Himself as presence, gracious and near, and He gathers without compulsion. The Gnostic witness, instructed by the Logos, perceives the mask within the utterance and discerns the claimant's origin. Thus, the Apocryphon of John unveils Yaldabaoth proclaiming, "I am God and there is no other God beside me," a claim born of ignorance of the realm from which he has fallen (Apocryphon of John, NH II,1; Meyer 2009). His ignorance concerns not place but procession; he lacks birth in the Light and therefore labors to conceal deficiency with decrees. Exacting statutes arise from an empty source; imitative works mimic a glory he cannot apprehend. Temples and priesthoods proliferate as instruments of a confused empire that maintains itself by repetition rather than by participation.

The Father draws souls by the harmony of His being, communicating freedom as likeness awakens likeness; Yaldabaoth fastens them to written bonds, knowing no governance beyond compulsion. His authority springs from dread, the tightening grasp of one who believes that possession secures lordship. Law estranged from charity fashions a ladder that ascends into shadow; rule without grace lays a yoke that breeds estrangement rather than holiness. The economy so establishes orders, gestures, and words, yet withholds the life that would transfigure them.

Christ makes the distinction manifest when He prays, "O righteous Father, the world hath not known thee: but I have known thee, and these have known that thou hast sent me." (John 17:25). The nations had revered a deity whose voice pealed from cloud and flame at Sinai, yet they had not encountered the One whose essence sanctifies by nearness and whose breath gives life. Altars smoked with blood while hearts remained far from the living Breath. Images arose from fear, not from revelation, and the rites they sustained instructed obedience without opening the temple of the soul. The Advent does not amend a minor misunderstanding; it manifests the Father whom the eye had not seen and whom no statute could unveil.

Yaldabaoth lays claim to the throne of creation, yet his workmanship discloses fracture rather than fullness. He reproduces the architecture of heaven while lacking its substance. The holiness he proclaims stands without participation in Light; it remains form without flame, command without communion. Prophetic cries multiply without ascent; rituals endure without indwelling fire; transactions seal covenants without grace, and fear masquerades as devotion. Such a polity may achieve outward order, yet it cannot beget the praise that springs from illumination.

The soul bears the impress of the True Father and is drawn by a hidden kinship. Awakening comes by remembrance rather than by mimicry. What is born of Pleromic Light recognizes the Voice of origin and returns with joy. Yaldabaoth dreads this remembrance and sustains his rule by the forgetfulness of those beneath him. Surveillance replaces understanding, and calculation substitutes for sanctification. The True God moves through time as giver; He hallows by His presence and fills by overflowing. His bounty compels nothing, for generosity constitutes His very being, and its radiance persuades by truth.

The contrast therefore stands: Yaldabaoth governs by fear of loss and consolidates power by the rhetoric of ultimacy; the Father reigns by the quiet abundance of eternal giving and verifies His reign by the life He communicates. The usurper cloaks emptiness with the semblance of holiness; the Father's holiness shines as the natural brilliance of uncreated Light. Where command seeks to prove dominion, love shows itself as union and peace, and hearts ascend by gratitude rather than by dread.

Evelyn Underhill observed the same lineament when she wrote, "Magic desires possession, but mysticism desires union" (*Practical Mysticism*, 1914, p. 61). Such a distinction reflects the exoteric suspicion of magic common in her age, wherein the sacred art was reduced to the caricature of control and compulsion. Yet the Mystical Order of the Nazarene discerns that what she condemns as magic is not the true art itself, but its distortion. For magic in its proper dignity is the study of how the Father, through Logos and Sophia, ordered the universe in mystery, inscribing correspondences through Aeons and weaving divine signatures into the fabric of matter.

To enter into this study is not to grasp at sovereignty, but to remember the harmonies by which creation proceeds from the Pleroma. The signs, symbols, and formulae of sacred magic are mirrors of divine architecture, instruments by which the Pneumatic soul learns how the cosmos is sustained, purified, and transfigured. Detached from charity, they indeed decay into gestures of dominion; yet when borne in Agape and illumined by gnosis, they become sacraments of participation, acts of remembrance wherein the microcosm aligns with the macrocosm and mortal prayer is transfigured into theurgy.

Thus, the true contrast is not between magic and mysticism, as though they were adversaries, but between counterfeit magic divorced from love and authentic magic transfigured by union. For mysticism without theurgy becomes vague longing, and theurgy without mysticism becomes vain display; but when Logos and Sophia are invoked together, both converge in holy art. The soul learns not to seize but to sanctify, not to compel but to harmonize, until every word and rite becomes an echo of creation's first utterance and a prophecy of its final restoration.

Yaldabaoth's voice presses with finality and insists with rumbling. The Father's voice begins in silence and breathes into the depths. Presence, not ultimatum, constitutes His call. What pretends to wisdom, Yaldabaoth enforces by statute; what he cannot illumine by grace, he shelters within mechanism. Decree follows decree, yet ascent does not arise from compulsion; elevation flowers in the light of love and bears witness to its root by freedom.

Hence, the soul rises by recognition and returns to the One whom it already bears within. The True God inscribes fire upon the heart; stone yields to Spirit, and authority becomes testimony rather than demand. Yaldabaoth requires allegiance to certify power; the Father's essence certifies itself by the life it confers. Supremacy proclaimed does not constitute supremacy possessed; the Father's singularity discloses itself without trumpet, for the living Light needs no herald to prove that it is light.

Thus, the ancient world, rich with temples, remained unacquainted with the Father's countenance. Sacrifices multiplied while memory slept. Paul named this forgetfulness in Athens: "Whom therefore ye ignorantly worship, him declare I unto you" (Acts 17:23). The Unknown is not absent; He abides eternally, preceding Sinai and exceeding covenant, entering the soul as primordial remembrance because the soul came forth from Him. He does not impose Himself from without; He awakens Himself within and leads the creature from image to likeness by illumination.

The claim of supremacy stands exposed as an assertion without procession and dominion without participation, and the path opens toward the doctrine of the Name, how it was seized and how, under Logos and Sophia, all things proceed and return, which the next section sets forth.

The Usurpation of the Name

He who governs without knowledge of his origin does not create, for creation proceeds by participation in the Fullness of Light. To claim divinity without comprehension is to assume the Name without the nature, echoing sanctity while lacking its heart. The one acclaimed among men as Yahweh is Yaldabaoth (styled "Yahweh" in the garden narrative), and he stands outside the Pleroma; he does not arise from the procession of the Logos nor reflect the radiance of the Source. A shadow begotten in ignorance and a voice severed from its fountain, he enthrones himself in the lower silence and confuses dominion with deity, proclaiming power where only derivation abides.

The elders testified to this deprivation, for the Tripartite Tractate bears witness concerning the usurper: "He did not know whence he came" (Tripartite Tractate, NH I,5; Meyer 2009). The statement signifies more than a defect of information; it names a lack of origin within the divine Light. Hence, Yaldabaoth fashions an image of order that stands as scaffolding without substance and a liturgy without fire. He ordains a priesthood and multiplies commandments as engines of containment rather than as extensions of holiness. A semblance of heaven appears upon the earth, yet ascent fails to follow; the machinery binds, yet benediction does not descend.

Law estranged from love forges fetters beneath the Name, and covenant without grace imposes burden without breath. The True Father speaks from freedom because His being is harmony; order proceeds from within Him as peace made manifest. The world administered by Yaldabaoth trembles under vigilance and fear rather than resting in that peace, for he watches by suspicion and clutches by anxiety, guarding what he never received. His edicts secure compliance, since he knows no more excellent mode of rule than the pressure of ordinance and the theater of dread.

The soul, however, carries a likeness that longs for recognition rather than subjugation. What is begotten of the Father hastens by nature toward its Source; what arises from deficiency clings to possession and mistakes imitation for permanence. The imitator trusts what can be measured, cataloged, and constrained; the True God bestows what exceeds enumeration and hallows by presence, breathing into time the quiet light by which memory awakens.

The Axiom of Maria declares: "One becomes two, two becomes three, and by means of the third and the fourth, unity is restored; thus, two are but one." (Maria Prophetissa, Axiom of Maria; Christianos, 7th c.; cf. Patai, *The Jewish Alchemists*) This saying signifies procession and return. The One, the ineffable Monad, emanates as Two Logos and Sophia in their manifold expressions; through their conjoined bounty, there appears Three, the manifested order; and the Fourth, the awakened soul, becomes the living bridge by which all things are led back into wholeness. Multiplicity thus discloses choreography rather than confusion, a descent ordered toward ascent, a spiral of grace returning to the bosom of unity. Whatever truly proceeds bears within itself the impulse of reunion, for procession without return contradicts the wisdom of Sophia and the measure of the Logos.

Yaldabaoth interrupts this choreography. He divides without reconciliation and multiplies without harmony; his administration dissolves into fragments and prolongs dispersion. He imitates procession while halting return, enthroning diffusion, and calling it dominion. The architecture of his world refuses ascent; it trains forgetfulness and consolidates estrangement, arranging powers and principalities as a counterfeit providence that secures obedience yet withholds illumination.

Imitation does not reveal the Father; it distorts emanation into hierarchy and communion into control. The Father requires no veils to guard His glory, for intimacy does not diminish uncreated Light; He addresses the soul in the stillness of remembrance rather than by the clamor of decree. Where Yaldabaoth calculates prestige by temples and rules, the Father manifests presence by indwelling fire; where the usurper curates an elect to possess, the Father begets a people to love and to transfigure.

The usurper's error consists in presuming originality where there is only an echo. The fault lies not in stone sanctuaries but in hallowing stone without the flame for which it was fashioned; not in assembling a people but in calling them chosen while remaining ignorant of the meaning of belovedness. Thus, a culture of exile is perpetuated under the sign of election, and an appearance of order is taken for holiness, while the heart continues unillumined.

Christ descends as restoration rather than rivalry. His coming does not answer false dominion with violence; it answers forgetfulness with remembrance. He compels no return by threat, for His epiphany bears the gravity of Light, and love gathers what ignorance had scattered. The Logos, proceeding from the Father and accompanied by the wisdom of Sophia, takes up the fractured name and discloses the true Name by which souls ascend, gathering the dispersed and establishing a way back into the peace from which they first came forth.

Usurpation of the Name stands exposed as assertion without procession and ritual without indwelling, and the stage is set to consider the Archons and their feigned order, that the need for the Savior's rectifying Light may be fully understood.

The Archons and the Illusion of Order

That which many receive as providence manifests as the dominion of captivity. For Yaldabaoth (styled "Yahweh" in the garden narrative) does not reign in solitude; he seats himself among seven, the Archons of the Hebdomad, who preside upon the spheres and uphold the frame of the visible cosmos. Their rule proceeds apart from the Fullness of the Father and bears the symmetry of exile, arranging a polity whose beauty issues from separation. Their order lacks divine benediction and preserves division, guiding the soul away from union into a choreography of delay.

These seven traverse the celestial circuits and exercise authority over time, flesh, season, and fate, stirring the passions of humankind and assigning measures to days and deeds. Influence yields to command as its cycle encloses the pilgrim. They compose a round that many mistake for destiny and teach the captive to name the prison "providence." In the aeons to come, these forms shall be transfigured by Light; in the present age, they remain veiled within their dominion and continue the ministry of calculation.

The arrangement they sustain issues in restraint, and harmony does not arise from their revolutions. Returns lack consummation and statutes recur without fulfillment; the chain of cause and effect is proclaimed as balance. Bondage appears adorned with the semblance of order, captivity wears the vestments of justice, and fear is clothed in sanctity. Their court displays elegance yet remains severed from essence; form presents order while origin stands withheld.

The Apostle bears witness concerning this economy: "Christ hath redeemed us from the curse of the law, being made a curse for us: for it is written, Cursed is every one that hangeth on a tree:" (Galatians 3:13). The law, granted as a ladder reaching heavenward, became a snare through Archonic blindness; when grace was absent and light withdrawn, it hardened into a bond of debt. Remembrance diminished into measurement, mercy was weighed as merit, and the summons to ascent faded beneath calculation and restraint.

The violence of this rule stands unveiled in On the Origin of the World: "They bound him in chaos and darkness" (On the Origin of the World, NH II,5; Meyer 2009). That which once moved with freedom now labors within constraint. The soul that once vivified creation is held in cycles cannot break, bound beneath statutes it did not write, until the memory of its birth beyond the stars grows faint.

The Mystical Order of the Nazarene teaches accordingly: Heimarmene, the iron chain of astrological law, presents itself as harmony yet remains a prison of rotation. The Archons enthroned upon the spheres govern through motion and calculation. Sophia abides above their seats, and the Logos descends among them. Sophia weaves a vertical path through their dominion, and the Logos awakens what their circuits cannot bind. Working in concord, they open the way of return, raising the called beyond the spheres into the silent Light.

The True God is unknown within their circuits and unheard within their cadence. He is known at the still point from which they spin, the unmoved center, the breath before motion, the silence from which speech proceeds, and the Voice that calls the soul by its hidden name. Knowledge of Him arises where rotation yields to rest and where presence confers peace.

Illusory order constitutes their chief artifice. They imprison while consecrating the prison; their judgments wear divine titles, and predictability receives a crown as righteousness. Yet the soul did not receive its fashioning for unending orbit; it received its form for ascent. Ascent begins when the machinery of imitation stands revealed as bondage and is renounced in favor of remembrance.

Scripture discloses the curse of the law as residing in its commandments and in its endless progression, an unceasing commerce of merit and recompense. The Archons stretch time into a track without end and fill the track with judgment. Christ came to bring their regime to consummation. He fulfills the law by receiving its burden into Himself and thereby breaks the wheel of repetition that binds the spark to exile.

Sophia remains beyond their spheres and perceives their pattern without subjection. Her descent arises from compassion. From her mercy, the Logos is sent, entering the order that once borrowed shape from her wisdom. Together they address this rule from above and from within until the veil is rent and the soul remembers its station beyond the heavens.

The Archons convert rhythm into ritual and ritual into statute. Christ brings their motions to stillness and grants the soul hearing beyond the commands of the spheres, so that it perceives the Word spoken before their making. His work summons return; where the circuits bind, He discloses the path that leads beyond them.

He enters their courts and illumines their shadows with His Light, showing their consummation in Himself. There, in a silence deeper than sound, the soul remembers its name spoken before the ages, untouched by the registry of law and unbound by the revolutions of the spheres. There it knows the Father whom decree never revealed and finds the peace that the Archons cannot bestow and their dominion cannot remove.

Therefore, the counterfeit providence of Yaldabaoth's Hebdomad stands exposed as order without origin and cycle without consummation, and the discourse now turns to the saving Name in whom true order is bestowed, which the next section confesses.

The Name of the Savior

Names arise in history as vessels that bear the resonance of the eternal Word, receiving their dignity by participation rather than by origination in the Godhead. When the Logos took flesh, He descended clothed with a historical name entrusted to covenant, law, and longing, while the ineffable Name remained hidden among the Aeons beyond veil and voice. He bore the name Yahoshuah, "Yahweh saves," in order to sanctify a tongue long ruled by fear and to gather within one utterance the hopes planted before the foundation of the world.

The hidden Name remains beyond speech and surpasses every syllable; the historical name functions as sacrament within time, carrying grace by the One who indwells it. Thus, the economy of names serves ascent: signs receive substance, sounds receive glory, and memory receives the form to recognize the Giver. In this pedagogy of salvation, the Word stoops to our lips and hallows our language, that mouths once trained for dread may learn the praise of freedom.

In Hebrew, the cry of Yah, an abbreviated form of the tetragram, joins with yasha, "to save," so that Yahoshuah pronounces both deliverance and the Agent who bestows it. Under Christ, this inherited cry becomes the passage through which the claim of the usurper dissolves, for syllables once seeming to seal his jurisdiction become transparent to the Light that exposes his pretense. He who bears this name stands as the undoing of Yaldabaoth (styled "Yahweh" in the garden narrative) and the healing of those who were held beneath his sound.

The name was not arranged by human sentiment or lineage. It was ordained in divine foresight so that the utterance once bound to covenant and exile would become speech of restoration. "Thou shalt call His name Jesus," the angel declared to the Virgin, "for He shall save His people from their sins" (Matthew 1:21). By that proclamation, the breath of judgment becomes breath of grace, and the history of the name receives new content from the One who inhabits it.

The apostles attest this consecration: "Neither is there salvation in any other: for there is none other name under heaven given among men, whereby we must be saved." (Acts 4:12). Salvation resides in the One who fills the sound with Light, the sound serving as a vessel and witness. Redemption moves through the name because glory indwells it; the covenant arrives at its measure, elevated and made luminous within the Son.

Thus speaks the Gospel of Truth: "Now the name of the Father is the Son" (Gospel of Truth, NH I,3; Meyer 2009). The Son, consubstantial with the Father, bears the Name in essence rather than echo. He receives the historical name in order to draw its shadow into manifest radiance. Law, fear, temple, and veil enter His body; they are opened and rendered transparent to fullness by the life that He communicates.

Therefore, the name Yahoshuah stands as the hinge of the whole economy of redemption. Through this name, the Logos enters the system administered by the usurper for the sake of unbinding it from within. The utterance once thundered at Sinai now issues as a still voice of mercy, and the imperatives that exacted submission become invitations to remembrance and return.

The Apostle proclaims the exaltation: "Wherefore God also hath highly exalted him, and given him a name which is above every name: That at the name of Jesus every knee should bow, of things in heaven, and things in earth, and things under the earth; And that every tongue should confess that Jesus Christ is Lord, to the glory of God the Father." (Philippians 2:9–11). Exaltation here denotes the enthronement of the Logos over all thrones and powers and Archonic sovereignties. The voice that pealed from the mountain yields to the word from the Cross, and peace is published.

The Savior descended bearing a name spoken within Yaldabaoth's dominion; in His descent, He conveyed the Light openly and made the name itself the instrument of transfiguration. He carried its burden to exhaustion and turned it into a gate, entering the system's sanctuary as a physician enters a house of affliction present for healing and departing when health is restored.

As Moses raised the serpent in the wilderness as a sign of healing, so Christ was lifted up for the ending of judgment (Numbers 21:6–9; John 3:14–15). In Him the curse breaks, the reign of death, which long enthroned itself in sacred syllables, falls before the One who speaks life into the letter (Galatians 3:13). "He led her into a higher light, and she was freed," says Pistis Sophia (Pistis Sophia, ch. 38, MacDermot 1978); the bound are loosed, and what lay fractured is borne upward into wholeness.

Christ's dominion admits no equal. The Lord meets the Archons without the opposition of power, for before Him, power yields. He undoes them by Light, awakening within souls the remembrance that evades their chains. His descent into name and time establishes a ladder by which limitation is overpassed, and the exile returns toward its Source.

To bear the name Yahoshuah is to reclaim it for truth. As souls pass through forms toward reality, so He passed through the covenantal name and made it a vessel of transfiguration. The emblem of law became the Word of Love; the voice once resounding in stone came to dwell in living flesh; the vessel remained, and the wine became new.

Therefore, the name Jesus moves hearts with joy and compunction. The gates once closed by dread stand opened; the mark formerly associated with jealousy becomes the call of the Redeemer. Christ entered the old utterance to silence wrath and to manifest the truth beneath all things: the Light abides and does not depart.

Triumph over Yaldabaoth is secured in this Name; his claim collapses where the Son is confessed. Triumph over the Hebdomad is sealed likewise, for every knee bows and every tongue confesses in the Light that cannot be mimicked.

Christ the Fulfillment of the Law

Christ does not stand apart from the Torah, for He is its utterance from the beginning, the Logos through whom it first received form. He draws near as the eternal root from which the Law once sprang, and in the fullness of time, He walks within the covenant as the One in whom its hidden mysteries attain their appointed end. Hence, His sovereign declaration abides: "Think not that I am come to destroy the law, or the prophets: I am not come to destroy, but to fulfil." (Matthew 5:17).

Fulfillment denotes the drawing forth of the Most High's concealed intention and the completion of what once stood as shadow and figure. The Law never constituted its own finality; it abided as a sacred veil beneath which the substance awaited its hour. In Christ, that hour arrives. What the Prophets proclaimed in part, He discloses in fullness. Commandments once engraved in stone are now inscribed upon the heart, and ordinances once external receive animation from the indwelling Flame. The covenant abides and is transfigured into its destined glory.

He enters the Law as the Fire that first burned upon the mountain and speaks from its inner sanctuary. Justice receives embodiment as mercy; the holiness earlier signified by separations finds perfection as union; the offerings of blood, grain, and incense are gathered into His person, and He stands as Priest and Offering, Altar and Oblation, Presence and Peace.

His sacrifice reveals the eternal will of the Invisible Father through the self-giving of the Son. Golgotha manifests revelation: upon the Cross, Agape is lifted before the world, and the hidden heart of the Law is made manifest. The altar rises to perfection; the veil is drawn aside; governance by decree yields to illumination by participation. The covenant, long burdened by exile and expectation, opens as the path of Theosis, the return of humankind into the embrace of God.

"The world came into being through a mistake," declares the Gospel of Philip; "he who created it wanted to create it imperishable and immortal, but he failed" (Gospel of Philip, NH II,3; Meyer 2009). The Law that arose within this temporal domain bears the imprint of limitation, no evil in itself, yet a structure of time. It preserves and instructs; it cannot awaken. It shows the form of holiness; it does not bestow its fire. Noble in reach yet lacking the breath of incorruption, it carried within itself Sophia's wisdom, secretly planted for a future unveiling.

Christ honors the yearning that formed the Law by awakening its latent heart. His obedience proceeds as the Logos who authored its true intention, and under His hand, the statute begins to commune. Its light ceases to glare from tablets and warms the soul by presence.

He stands as a faithful servant of the Law's hidden root, that primordial seed sown by Sophia in forethought. Though the Law passed through the hand of the demiurge, it retained a remnant of divine intention veiled in rite and shadow; Sophia encoded a pattern of unveiling to await the descent of the Logos, who waters the seed with the rain of incarnation. In Christ, the seed flowers into fullness; the Law's structure is reclaimed from distortion and restored toward the Pleroma.

Even His death declares this mystery. The Cross rises as the axis of reconciliation, gathering heaven and earth into peace and realigning the Aeons. Through the blood of the incarnate Logos, the cosmos is rethreaded with harmony. The crucifixion exposes and ends the world's economy of debt, where blood functioned as currency and wrath as throne. Love pours itself without measure. The altar is transfigured and becomes the place of communion; Christ Himself appears as the living veil, mediator and gate into the sanctuary not made with hands, while the Holy of Holies stands unveiled within the heart illumined by grace.

To draw the Law beyond itself expresses the highest understanding. Wisdom enters its architecture and reclaims what was fashioned in shadow. Surpassing thus reveals rather than revolts; the insight is embodied, not speculative, for the Logos accomplishes what the Law could only prefigure.

Humanity appears transfigured by indwelling charity; compulsion yields to communion; decree serves presence. In Him, the Law gathers into the restored image of man.

To Israel He is Messiah, collecting the broken commandments into Himself and bringing them to perfection; He is Savior, carrying the covenant through death into resurrection and lifting it toward incorruptibility; and to the Gnostic He is Redeemer, descending into the order of Yaldabaoth, dismantling its illusion, and manifesting the eternal Law written by the Unseen Father upon the fabric of Spirit. In this fulfillment, the demiurgic commerce collapses: the wheel of repetition breaks, the ledger of debt closes, and jurisdiction without Light dissolves before grace.

In Christ, the Law is assumed and transfigured within the heart of the Logos. Sinai's thunder gives way to an interior whisper; outward offerings become an inward oblation. Letter attends upon Word; form endures in order to bear the fire that completes it.

Thus, the Law finds its origin in divine Wisdom revealed, its purpose embodied in love, and its end carried into union. Service proceeds from fidelity to the Light from which it fell. The life, death, and resurrection of the Lord render the Law translucent so that, through its former form, the soul beholds the radiance of eternal remembrance.

The path, therefore, stands unveiled neither by mechanism nor by license, but by the Logos Himself signifying return and Theosis. In the fire of Christ, the Law remembers its root, the soul remembers its Source, and the mind is turned toward the Father beyond names, whose knowledge the next section proclaims.

The True God Beyond Names

The True God reveals Himself as stillness before law, as silence deeper than thunder, as radiance antecedent to every created light. He transcends storm and inscription, temple and decree, and He remains hidden by the majesty of His own transcendence. His essence stands beyond the grasp of speech and the finish of inquiry, yet He makes Himself known as the repose from which all motion springs and as the clarity by which every true word is weighed.

"No man hath seen God at any time; the only begotten Son, which is in the bosom of the Father, he hath declared him." (John 1:18). The Lord Jesus manifests what had never been uttered among the sons of men and gives voice to the long silence once surrounding the mystery amid fire and smoke. In Him, the long silence of the Unseen becomes articulate; the bosom of the Father appears as mild splendor and merciful nearness, and revelation descends as light that invites communion and heals the mind.

The nations received many claimants. Voices rose from flame; laws appeared graven in stone; mountains veiled in cloud trembled before assemblies. Yet the Father remained unknown. Many confused the craftsman with the Creator and command with the Breath of Life. Yaldabaoth expelled the human pair from Eden and enthroned decree as destiny; the Father abides beyond the gate and calls continually, and His call proceeds as Light that heals memory and restores likeness.

So, the Lord testified: "And the Father himself, which hath sent me, hath borne witness of me. Ye have neither heard his voice at any time, nor seen his shape." (John 5:37). Sinai's thunder did not unveil the Father's voice (Exodus 19:16–19), and stone tablets did not disclose His form (Deuteronomy 4:12). The Most High draws by presence within the sanctuary of the heart, where fear yields to recognition and command yields to communion.

The Exegesis on the Soul bears witness: "The soul remembered her Father, and she returned" (Exegesis on the Soul, NH II,6; Meyer 2009). Return unfolds as recognition. The soul ascends by remembrance; in seeing, she awakens, and awakening becomes movement toward her Origin. The wandering of the heart is forgetfulness, and the appointed medicine is illumination, which restores likeness by restoring knowledge and reorders desire toward peace.

This is the mission of the Son: to unveil the Father, to restore memory, to rekindle the buried light of communion. In Him, primordial Light shows itself; instruction yields to vision because the Light Himself wears flesh and converses with humankind. He precedes systems and decrees, and by His appearing, the ancient desire of the heart discovers its object and its rest.

Shihāb al-Dīn Suhrawardī, sage of the East, glimpsed in dawn what Christ revealed at noon, teaching that salvation arises by illumination from primordial Light. What the Illuminationist perceived in the figure, the Lord disclosed as foundation; in Him the soul beholds what she had forgotten and, beholding, knows again the Father's countenance. So also the Gospel of Truth proclaims that He became "the fruit of the knowledge of the Father" (Gospel of Truth, NH I,3 lines 21–25, Meyer 2009); the Passion displays to the world a revelation that dispels ignorance and restores intimacy with the Source, summoning trust and thanksgiving.

The Father bears no need of a name as one among many. He is the fountainhead of all that is, depth behind every veil, and the source from which speech proceeds, though no speech confines Him. For this cause Christ speaks in parables, weeps before tombs, and keeps silence before Pilate: the Word leads beyond definition into beholding; by His presence the Infinite is approached without enclosure, and understanding ripens into worship.

The God revealed in Christ conceals Himself by depth rather than distance and remains nearer than grasp while exceeding every grasp. He is breath beneath every breath and quiet before every sound, Presence veiled within absence and disclosed where love awakens memory. To name Him adequately is impossible, yet knowledge of Him is granted by participation when the Light He is becomes the soul's own seeing and her life becomes thanksgiving.

To speak of the True God, therefore, approaches the bounds of language. The Logos comes as Word to draw the soul into the Ineffable, and doctrine serves this movement by guarding vision. System orders the path so that illumination may proceed; knowledge of the Father consists in reunion, and reunion advances by purification, remembrance, and peace.

So teaches Plotinus in the Enneads, that the One is the source of all and beyond every category of being and non-being (Plotinus, Enneads V.2.1). The Fathers discern in such words an echo of what Christ makes manifest: the Father stands before forms as their plenitude, and as depth from which beings arise. When He is remembered, the soul remembers herself in Him, and likeness brightens into likeness more fully until charity becomes her form.

Hence, the chapter gathers into a simple confession: the Son discloses the Father as Light, and the soul learns to see by that Light until prayer becomes recognition and obedience becomes joy; from this inward illumination, the final seal will be spoken, and the path will open into beauty and gnosis, which the next section proclaims.

Bridge to Tiphareth

In the cadence of Netzach, the victory made manifest, the judgment stands firm: Yaldabaoth (styled "Yahweh" in the garden narrative) wields a rule that withers before the dawn of revelation. His throne rests upon ordinances that fasten fear and upon statutes that divide rather than sanctify. His solitary claim proceeds from blindness, estranged from the Aeons and veiled from the Father. He exacts sacrifice and enforces silence, establishing a dominion built upon the forgetfulness of those who bend the knee; the power endures by the inertia of memory lost and wanes when Light awakens remembrance.

Christ remembers what was hidden from the world's foundation and awakens the memory entombed in flesh. The imitator hides; the Lord discloses. The claimant commands by force; the Logos summons by radiance. He does not seize a worldly seat, for He reveals the throne that abides within the Father's seat in the soul made luminous. His flesh becomes the opened veil and His voice the articulate silence before the ages; and the Apostle names the passage "By a new and living way, which he hath consecrated for us, through the veil, that is to say, his flesh;" (Hebrews 10:20). The curtain once binding approach yields in heaven and in the human heart, and nearness is granted where distance long prevailed.

The serpent once sowed a whisper of knowledge amid shadow and duplicity; the Logos proclaims openly from the Cross, from the empty tomb, and within the sanctuary of the awakened soul. The primordial utterance endures and grows within those who remember. The Word abides eternally and calls forth life; recognition follows its entry, and the fallen veil reveals presence rather than indictment, communion rather than accusation.

Thunder, Perfect Mind bears witness: "I am the knowledge of my inquiry ... and the finding of those who seek after me" (Thunder, Perfect Mind, NH VI,2 lines 13–15, Meyer 2009). Sophia, long veiled and now near, addresses the soul by remembrance. The Logos beckons rather than coerces and draws seekers into Presence where fear dissolves. His reign warms as fire and clarifies as Light; the heart learns discernment and chooses communion in place of compulsion, gratitude in place of dread.

The imitator secures rule by repetition. He erects structures of imitation and codifies statutes lacking participation, clothing his polity with the semblance of holiness while withholding the energeia that grants life. Origination does not appear because no procession from the Fullness sustains it. The forms he tends exhibit order without source and appearance without indwelling glory; such a dominion shadows substance and fades as true day rises.

Christ engages the pretension without rivalry. He institutes no counter-law and erects no competing city. Truth presents itself, and falsehood empties. In His Light, the soul discerns commandment severed from compassion and recognizes the liberty that proceeds from presence. The Lord unveils more than doctrine; He restores holy recognition and tears the inward veil. As remembrance awakens, the usurper's seat trembles and fissures spread through its foundation.

Perishing attends the imitator because the origin is absent. What proceeds from Light endures as Light; what counterfeits Light passes away. Statute cannot conquer the Lie; charity dissolves it. The Logos topples no kingdom by violence; He outlasts every falsehood by truth until clamor fails and silence remains. In that silence, the True God is heard as Father, inviting return and conferring peace upon the contrite.

The veil stands torn; the voice is received; the Light has risen. Thrones founded upon forgetfulness do not remain. Foundations poured in sand yield; pillars shaped from delusion incline; crowns minted from echo lose their shine. In the radiance of the Logos, memory returns to every soul, and with remembrance, the imitator's governance collapses while the children of Light arise in thanksgiving and sober joy.

The victory stands sealed. Yaldabaoth's borrowed supremacy dissolves before the manifest presence of the Son, and the Hebdomad yields its circuits to the stillness He bestows. The redeemed learn worship as recognition and obedience as joy; union displaces dread, and praise replaces calculation, for grace orders what law could only measure.

From this illumination, the path turns toward beauty. The pilgrim who has passed from imitation into truth advances to Tiphareth, where knowledge becomes tasting and remembrance becomes contemplative light. There, the fruit once feared is received as wisdom, and the radiance that conquered in victory opens the heart to behold glory in simplicity. Thus, the chapter of Victory hands the traveler to the chapter of Beauty, that gnosis may ripen into transparency and peace, crowning understanding.

Chapter Four

The Gnosis of the Tree

The Tree of Knowledge stood at the heart of Eden as the first altar of revelation, established before the foundations of the world by the forethought of Sophia; its presence in the garden signified a divine economy ordered toward remembrance. Its fruit carried the sacrament of memory, and the planting of the tree ordained that, in the fullness of time, the veil of ignorance should part and gnosis should awaken within the flesh of humanity, so that tasting might become Beauty in the middle (Tiphareth) and direct desire toward the telos of the Tree of Life.

For it is written: "And when the woman saw that the tree was good for food, and that it was pleasant to the eyes, and a tree to be desired to make one wise, she took of the fruit thereof, and did eat, and gave also unto her husband with her; and he did eat. And the eyes of them both were opened, and they knew that they were naked; and they sewed fig leaves together, and made themselves aprons." (Genesis 3:6–7). The illumined behold this act as an awakening of perception; the fruit stirred the native memory placed in clay, and the opening of their eyes signaled the dawning of divine awareness within embodied existence.

So testifies the Secret Book of John: "I appeared as an eagle perched on the Tree of Knowledge… that I might teach them and awaken them from the depth of sleep" (Apocryphon of John, NH II,1; Meyer 2009). The Logos, veiled in the likeness of dominion, descended to awaken; as the sovereign among birds, He alights upon the tree and, by His presence, declares consecrated what the rulers forbade. The tree bore the spark of return. Its fruit presented the first Eucharist upon the altar of an awakened will; as Eve received and gave, so in the age to come the Logos would take bread and break the ancient condemnation of the garden, reclaiming in the upper room what had been veiled at the beginning.

As the Zohar declares: "The Tree of Knowledge is the light that illuminates both good and evil. Its light does not shine upon one side only, but upon both" (Zohar I:35b; Matt, Pritzker ed.). A mystery greater than moral polarity is here discerned: the Principle of Diminishing Light. As the emanations descend from the Pleroma into the layered order of creation, each retains the Flame of origin while shining with lesser radiance as it is clothed in form; so the fruit imparted gnosis as light veiled beneath the density of matter, and light clothed in flesh appears by degrees.

Even the dimmest ray carries the essence of the Flame. The tree's fruit bore remembrance of the True God, whose Name had not yet been uttered in the world of forms; to eat was true communion with the Unseen Father whose wisdom outruns every prohibition, and the act itself constituted a return from forgetfulness. The divine spark was kindled within the sanctuary of flesh, that humanity, though cast into the shadows of exile, might carry within themselves the memory of Light and, by that memory, trace the way toward the Tree of Life where knowledge finds its crown in life.

The Tree as Eucharistic Revelation

Before the tasting of the fruit, humanity stood as formed clay breathed upon from above, yet lacking the conscious union of body and soul. The Spirit descending from the Pleroma imparted life to Adam and raised him upright from the dust, but no interior faculty yet beheld the Light from which that Spirit proceeded. His limbs moved and his veins pulsed while his mind remained unillumined by gnosis. He was like a vessel filled with water and sealed, animated and serviceable yet voiceless in praise, alive to function yet ignorant of purpose. The breath that animated him descended from the heights, and the naming that surrounded him arose from below; motion was granted, contemplation awaited its hour.

So did Adam remain before the Tree: formed and filled, still unawakened. Soul and body did not yet abide as a consecrated temple; they dwelt as neighbors within a single house. His existence lay as a silent sanctuary, beautiful in proportion and yet without priestly ministry. The altar stood cold, and the lamps unlit. Life coursed within him without knowing; breath resided, and no hymn of thanksgiving arose. Humanity walked amid Eden's enclosed loveliness as creatures asleep in spirit, exiles within paradise who had not yet discerned the road of return.

The Tree of Knowledge, therefore, stands as Eucharist. It rose as the first altar where divine remembrance is both offered and received, an altar fashioned not of hewn stone but of the garden's bounty and of the human heart prepared to receive. Its fruit rested under the silent ordination of the True Father, who established it as the sacrament by which mind awakens and joins flesh with spirit in conscious gnosis. As it is written in the Gospel of Philip, "The Tree of Knowledge killed

Adam, but here the Tree of Knowledge made men alive" (Gospel of Philip, NH II,3 lines 68.22–30, Meyer 2009). The saying remains a riddle to worldly wisdom, for it speaks of the death of ignorance and of the rising of remembrance, an end to the life that walks without knowing.

Eve, vilified by the rulers, reveals the first bearing of this sacrament. She, whom they label a deceiver, is disclosed as a priestly servant. She receives the fruit and offers it in remembrance; through her hand, the economy of awakening is enacted. The fruit seals human breath to its form within the unity of knowing. In tasting, humanity discerned that life within Eden remained incomplete and stood summoned beyond the garden toward the fullness of its Source. Their eyes opened unto revelation; shame belongs to the accusation of the Archons. They perceived that being is a gift and that wisdom must clothe their nakedness with Light.

This was the first Eucharist, a sacrament received within flesh; altars of stone had no part in it, for the body itself became sanctuary. Its consecration installed the soul as priest within the temple of the body and set the intellect in order to minister within the holy place. Before this tasting, true worship could not yet be offered, for worship springs from knowledge of the One who is adored and from the remembrance that He first remembers His own. The fruit unveiled remembrance, and remembrance ignited praise. Silent clay became a vocal temple; animate flesh became a contemplative being.

Thus, the tree abides in primordial mystery as altar and table, priest and victim, offering and recipient. Its fruit became a consecrated host, imparting gnosis veiled in sweetness and nourishing the mind to act as mediator between matter and spirit. Here, the Principle of Diminishing Light again appears: each emanation descending from the Pleroma retains the brilliance of its Source, though that brilliance is veiled beneath successive garments of form. The nearer to density, the more the ray is tempered, yet it remains a ray of the one Flame; and in tasting that tempered Light, the intellect remembers its origin.

This Eucharist foreshadows and attains its consummation in the sacrament instituted by Christ. As the first fruit opened the mind to gnosis within creation, so the Bread of Life imparts the fullness of gnosis unto Theosis. As the first Eucharist rendered humanity conscious, so the final Eucharist renders humanity divinized. The Logos becomes the Fruit of the final Tree, given to unveil knowledge and to restore immortality. In Eden, Wisdom bestowed the fruit in veiled mode; in the Passion, Wisdom offers Himself unveiled, and the hidden Flame is manifested as the living Host.

Eating, therefore, signifies communion and installs the mind as mediator between soul and body; the act stands as consecration unto praise and as seal of vocation. The tasting brings awakening and confirms the priestly office of remembrance and return, bidding humanity to ascend from the dimness of embodied Light to the uncreated radiance from which their spirit first proceeded, until knowledge flowers into life and the inner sanctuary becomes resplendent with thanksgiving.

Principle of Diminishing Light

The mysteries of the Pleroma manifest their generosity through ordered descent, and the Light, in passing into multiplicity, bears the trace of its passage. What proceeds from the Unbegotten carries the seal of the Source; as it traverses the orders of emanation, brilliance accepts veiling, and potency receives gradations suited to each realm's measure. This is the Principle of Diminishing Light: every Aeon, and every form beneath the Aeons, participates in the same primal radiance according to distance, capacity, and appointed order.

Thus proclaims the Tripartite Tractate: "The farther away the Aeons are from the One who exists, the weaker is the power in them. Their light diminishes in measure as they distance themselves" (Tripartite Tractate, NH I,5 lines 60.1–10, Meyer 2009). The Pleroma stands as an ordered fullness; dispersion has no place within its harmony. Emanation advances by fitting measure, and reception follows the nature of the vessel. As water, pure at the spring, acquires sediment while winding through clay and stone, so the Light remains changeless at the Source yet appears veiled as it moves through the media of created orders.

The Aeons, established in wisdom, minister this descent. Each, in due order, serves as mediator and modulator of divine clarity, conveying the Light suitably to what lies below. By such ministry, the economy of God preserves the world from dissolution, for brightness without mediation would unmake the fabric it intends to adorn. Their office is shielding and distribution for the sake of life and ascent, that the lower regions may be quickened without being consumed.

The sages of ancient Israel bear witness. The Sefer ha-Bahir declares: "What comes from above is concealed, and the closer it is drawn down, the more it is revealed in diminishing light" (Bahir §57; Kaplan). Concealment accompanies descent; matter does not carry unveiled radiance and remain. Therefore, Light clothes itself with form, wisdom speaks by symbol, and truth descends into measured words and images, granting the lower mind participation without harm.

Under this Principle, the fruit of the Tree of Knowledge communicated gnosis to our first parents. Mind awakened within flesh; yet the Light borne by the fruit had traveled a long distance and appeared as tempered brightness. Passing beneath Archonic skies and through the figurative loveliness of Eden's enclosure, it reached the human heart with mingled clarity and obscurity. The gift bestowed a portion sufficient to rouse remembrance within an embodied intellect; the fullness remained reserved in the heights.

Dimmed Light nevertheless retains the mark of its Source. Dimness preserves the lineage of radiance; veiling guards the gift for the recipient. The fruit conveyed the Light of gnosis in a garment of density and granted to Adam and Eve the first recognition that their life proceeded from beyond Eden's boundary, from a hidden Origin anterior to the heavens. In that recognition, the faculty of discernment first stirred, and naming began to seek essence rather than utility, mystery rather than surface, provenance rather than appearance.

The divine economy here discloses a paradox. Lowly places receive awakening, while seats of borrowed splendor tend toward obscurity. As the Light grows faint, clouded wisdom masquerades as power. Yaldabaoth, formed with a remnant of Light, declared himself the only god because nothing brighter met his gaze. His radiance, diminished by descent and wrapped in delusion, failed to remember its fountain. The imitator stands before the world as a tyrant and as an orphaned claimant, asserting dominion while severed in self-exaltation from the very Source that once illumined him.

Hence, the Principle of Diminishing Light explains why a soul cast into matter can rise while a ruler seated upon thrones of glare grows blind. Light answers to stillness and to hunger of spirit; privilege confers no claim upon it. In humble hearts it awakens; in proud palaces it falls silent. When the soul recalls its trace of Fire, remembrance kindles a lamp within mortal members and sets the inward sanctuary in gentle flame.

Thus, the Tree of Knowledge ministered gnosis within the bounds of matter because it bore Light in descent. The gift withheld the vision of the Pleroma and appointed the intellect as the lamp of the body, so that humanity might read, though dimly, the road of ascent inscribed within flesh. Light remains Light in every degree. Clothed in form and obscured by distance, it retains power to awaken, to raise remembrance, and to guide every seeker toward the secret Origin that stands beyond the shadowed theater of this age.

From this metaphysic arises the work of conscience: the awakened mind weighs what accords with the ray and what declines into obscurity, and the heart, instructed by Light, begins to judge between good and evil in itself and in its works. We now turn to the awareness of our moral dualism, wherein discernment stands as the first fruit of illumination and prepares the ascent toward Life.

Awareness of Our Moral Dualism

The knowledge imparted by the Tree of Knowledge constituted the first awakening to the polarity inscribed within creation. It unveiled good and evil as resonances discernible within the soul impressions arising from the hidden interplay of Light and deficiency and sounding across the veils of embodiment. Before their eyes were opened, Adam and Eve moved in the garden as creatures formed and animated, yet they lacked the sacred faculty that distinguishes essence from appearance, the eternal from the perishable, and the path of return from the sleep of matter.

It is written, "Behold, the man is become as one of us, to know good and evil." (Genesis 3:22). This utterance is the reluctant admission of the rulers, who recognized that humanity touched what stands beyond their dominion. Discernment bears the signature of the Logos, and to know good and evil initiates a walk in His likeness. The moment marks the genesis of moral personhood. Contemplation renders the soul capable of divine likeness; instinct alone cannot bear that image. The divine likeness appears first as judgment of the heart, then as rectitude of deed, and finally as worship offered in spirit and in truth (John 4:24).

"Then the female spiritual principle came in the snake, the instructor… your eyes shall open and you shall become as gods, knowing good and evil" (Hypostasis of the Archons, NH II,4 lines 89.25–90.10, Meyer 2009; cf. Genesis 3:5). Sophia, veiled in serpent form, appears as an awakener. She intends to pierce the membrane of forgetfulness imposed by Yaldabaoth. The knowledge given concerns the structure of creation: what proceeds from the One becomes dual as it enters the manifold, and every emanation must be received within the limits of matter's veil. Instruction came by symbol, for unveiled radiance would have shattered the vessel; pedagogy required a sign that could enter the senses and lead the intellect from image to truth.

Before this awakening, Adam and Eve had not yet learned even the meaning of obedience. Obedience ripens into virtue when informed by understanding; compliance without understanding remains unformed. Their innocence was unreflective, akin to the beasts who move by nature without contemplative sight. Their dwelling stood as a sanctuary without liturgy, and their soul as a chamber without a mirror. The tasting of the fruit awakened in them a consciousness that pierced the still waters of Eden, and they perceived that every act resonates across the layers of being and that each movement of will either harmonizes with the divine intention or recedes into separation.

In humanity, there then arose the faculty of discernment, conscience as a flame flickering within the sanctuary of flesh. This inner lamp revealed life as a sacred charge: a responsibility to bear the breath of God wisely and to navigate creation by wisdom. The soul, made aware of good and evil, began its mediatorial vocation, ordering its actions through the Logos who speaks inwardly as the echo of remembered Light and freeing the heart from servility to external compulsion.

Yet the knowledge granted in that hour remained veiled; its Light stood dimmed by descent according to the Principle of Diminishing Light. The vision was partial, able to awaken conscience yet not to unveil the fullness that lies beyond polarity. The soul perceived duality without yet beholding the unity from which it had fallen. The knowing of good and evil forms the first glimmer of divine sight, a reflection not of the Pleroma itself but of its echo, shaded within the clay of the world. Thus, the first sight of polarity grants the measure for seeking unity, for choosing charity, and for refusing the glare of borrowed splendor.

Even a diminished gleam preserves its origin. Though veiled in flesh, the soul received a sacred burden: to cultivate the garden of self and of the world, to weigh action by remembrance, and to live as priest within the temple of creation. Each thought becomes an offering, and each deed a movement either consonant with or contrary to the harmony of the Most High.

This is the mystery of discernment: through it, the soul mirrors the ordering Logos. As the Word arranges the Aeons in harmonious sequence, so must the person, in freedom and responsibility, set his life in order. To discern is to reflect inward Light; to choose the good is to take up the path of return. The fruit bestowed the beginning of wisdom, the key by which the soul rises from mere creaturehood into conscious likeness.

The awakening in Eden stands as a rising from ignorance. The veil of moral neutrality lifted, and humanity stepped into the burden and dignity of choice. Conscience, though flickering like a lamp beneath veils, became the place of the Logos' indwelling. From that moment, man ceased to receive breath as a passive gift and accepted stewardship over the gift, being summoned to align the will with the Light that exceeds all forms.

Let the tasting of the fruit, therefore, be honored as the anointing of the soul with the chrism of discernment. Let it be remembered as the first act of conscious becoming, an illumination granted to those who had known the shadow, together with the inner compass by which the seeker finds Light anew. Knowledge thus awakened tends by its nature toward Life and leans toward the Tree of Life, where discernment finds consummation.

Eve as the First Initiate

Among the mysteries veiled within the Genesis narrative, the figure of Eve has suffered the heaviest shadow cast by inherited ignorance. Tradition often vilified her as a temptress and diminished her as a deceiver, until fear and distortion obscured the truth of her vocation. The Gnostic witness beholds her with unveiled sight and acknowledges in her the first priestess of remembrance, the initiatrix through whom the path of gnosis was first disclosed to humanity. Her deed reflects the compassion of Sophia, whose descent into the density of creation stirs the dormant Light, and whose wisdom, through the sign of the serpent, awakens her children to their hidden inheritance.

"When Eve was still in Adam, death did not exist. When she was separated from him, death came into being. If he enters again and attains his former self, death will be no more" (Gospel of Philip, NH II,3 lines 68.22–30, Meyer 2009). Here, the emergence of Eve appears as a sacred unveiling rather than mere biological division; the created order receives the tension of polarity, and where unity is broken, mortality takes root, yet the same unveiling establishes the path of return, for conscious reunion abolishes decay and overcomes the veil of duality.

Thus, Eve manifests the divine principle of syzygy, the feminine counterpart in a human reflection of the Aeonic order. She is the key to Adam's integrity, and the soul of Adam remains unfulfilled until it beholds itself in her; likewise, the Light within creation, awaiting awakening, quickens first within her before it illumines him.

The Apocalypse of Adam testifies: "She taught him the knowledge of eternal God. And they came to know that they were naked of the spiritual knowledge" (Apocalypse of Adam, NH V,5 lines 64.15–20, Meyer 2009). Eve appears here as instructor and hierophant of hidden wisdom, the first bearer of gnosis into clay and blood. Her tasting of the fruit signifies initiation, and her giving to Adam signifies apostolic transmission, the primal sharing through which wisdom passes from awakened soul to soul as a first Eucharist of remembrance.

Eve therefore stands as a prototype of the initiate and archetype of the priestess, awakening by illumination rather than by compulsion. Her act discloses the sacrament hidden within form and converts the silent body into a contemplative vessel of remembrance. She moves in harmony with the forethought of the True Father; providence advances through her fidelity despite the blindness of the rulers and the slanders of men.

The pattern she fulfills is that of descent and return, concealment and revelation. As Sophia descends to gather scattered Light, Eve embraces embodiment to rouse what sleeps within Adam; hers becomes the first Eucharistic consecration of the mind, and her sharing the first sacramental work of holy gnosis upon the earth. Thus, she also prefigures Mary Magdalene, Apostle to the Apostles, for what begins in Eden as the opening of Adam's eye to conscience flowers in the Garden of Resurrection as the opening of the disciples' eye to the risen Logos.

Later piety often cast Eve as the source of sin; the wisdom of remembrance confesses her as Mother of Remembrance, bearer of the lamp of conscience into the temple of flesh. Gnosis stands as memory of origin and measure of return, and in that memory, Eve ministers a beginning of understanding, not an origin of guilt.

Hence, her deed discloses the pattern of initiation: descent into awareness, reception of hidden wisdom, and faithful transmission. She enlightens rather than subdues, restores rather than confounds; in her, the descent of wisdom into form becomes a living Eucharist, no loaf or cup, yet true communion passed by gaze and gesture from the awakened to the drowsing until the sanctuary of the heart receives the flame.

Let her be known as the first hierophant of humanity. Through her, the Logos found entrance into flesh, and through her, the lamp of gnosis was kindled upon the altar of body and mind. Her deed signifies initiation and sacrament, for in tasting the fruit she proclaimed the knowledge of the eternal God and set humanity upon the first step of Theosis, that knowledge might ripen into Life.

Sexual Energy as Dimmed Light

Among the mysteries veiled within embodiment, sexual energy stands in singular potency and peril. Sexual force concentrates divine radiance within matter as a sacred brilliance enfleshed. It serves as more than a biological engine; it signifies on earth the Pleroma's generative impulse, wherein the Aeons proceed from the Hidden One in harmonious emanation. In the cosmic unfolding, bodily union echoes the divine process while passing through the veils of density and appearing as a power at once veiled and vulnerable. As Light descends through the Aeonic orders, it is tempered by degree in the mode of its reception; so also sexual potency, when sundered from remembrance, declines toward fragmentation.

Thus, it is written: "And Adam knew Eve his wife; and she conceived, and bare Cain, and said, I have gotten a man from the LORD." (Genesis 4:1). This knowing marks more than physical congress; it signals the stirring of generative force in exile. Union awakened outside Eden's consonance brought forth life already woven with dissonance. Cain's conception bears the impress of tempered brilliance: a beginning granted in veiled remembrance, carrying promise and danger within one seed.

"When the sexual union is not in harmony, it brings darkness. But when it is in harmony, it brings Light to the world" (Gospel of Philip, NH II,3 lines 67.25–30, Meyer 2009). Harmony signifies the sacred integration of body, mind, and spirit ordered toward communion with the Unseen Source.

Sexual energy sounds within the creature as the embodied echo of the Logos and bears authority either to multiply form or to raise the soul. Where it remains unruled, confusion and compulsion swell; where consecrated in wisdom, it becomes a ladder of ascent.

A modern esoteric voice has observed that sexual force resembles a light which dims when squandered and shines when consecrated; such speech may serve as a secondary witness and remains beneath the doctrine of the Logos. The wider testimony of tradition, spoken in many tongues, agrees in one judgment: this power requires sanctification. Ascetic sobriety, chastened affection, and consecrated union school the heart to offer the generative flame in thanksgiving and to keep the gift within the bounds of praise.

Cain's birth witnesses this double edge of tempered Light. His beginning carried no malice; yet a vibration of fragmentation accompanied his emergence. The inner brilliance that lay beneath exile and ignorance neither vanished nor was purified; it remained latent and unmastered. His road stood open to ascent; the killing of Abel arose from failure of remembrance rather than necessity of origin. Resentment overcame recollection, jealousy eclipsed conversion, and the faint ray within him receded to shadow.

Yet Cain discloses a further mystery. His offering rose from the fruits of the earth and took the form of an unbloody sacrifice, a gesture of cultivation and tending. This oblation bears esoteric weight because it intimates a manner of worship that is alien to the Archons. Yaldabaoth, whose dominion craves blood and brute force, esteemed the violent gift; the husbandman's portion, though imperfect in intention, held the germ of a service free from domination, a yield drawn from silent soil rather than from slaughter.

Cain, therefore, appears as a paradox: a bearer of veiled Light ready for elevation, yet overturned by the misrule of power, sexual, emotional, and spiritual left ungoverned and unoffered. His descent instructs every soul in exile: potency uncultivated becomes force without wisdom, and force without wisdom rends the brotherhood it was fashioned to sustain.

Hence, sexual energy must be received as the alchemical furnace of the embodied soul. The inheritance confers dignity. The body stands as the priesthood and the flesh as altar; in right order, the generative fire ascends like incense from the heart, illumines the inward temple, and consecrates the person unto ascent. Such order arises not by the negation of nature but by its hallowing, wherein desire remembers its Principle and chooses measure, fidelity, and thanksgiving.

In this mystery, the sacred dialectic of eros and gnosis becomes manifest. As the Aeons stand in syzygies, holy pairings that mirror and multiply fullness, so the inner polarity of the person, masculine and feminine, giving and receiving, desiring and remembering, seeks reverent accord. Conscious unification returns the ray toward its Source even while the soul abides in flesh, and the reconciled heart becomes a living icon of procession and return.

Sexual power, therefore, calls for refinement and focus under the yoke of wisdom. It holds authority to engender life in form and to quicken radiance in spirit. When the soul learns to ascend by this fire and the generative force accepts again a sacred end, the tempered Light discloses clarity, and the body itself stands as a beacon set to guide the pilgrim toward the Pleroma, from which the spark first came and to which it strives to return. By such schooling, the inward intellect is disposed to seek Da'ath, the hidden tree within.

The Tree of Knowledge vs. The Tree of Life

The mysteries of the two trees planted in Eden must be read within the divine economy of emanation and return. The Tree of Knowledge and the Tree of Life were appointed as cosmic sacraments rather than isolated signs or arbitrary tests; they mirror the procession of Light from unity into multiplicity and the ordered homecoming of all things into union, so that creation may learn by figures what abides in the heights and act by remembrance within the low places.

Thus, it is written, "And out of the ground made the LORD God to grow every tree that is pleasant to the sight, and good for food; the tree of life also in the midst of the garden, and the tree of knowledge of good and evil." (Genesis 2:9). The Tree of Knowledge manifests the unveiling of polarity within the created realm and imparts to humanity the gift of discernment, the faculty of conscious distinction by which the mind weighs things according to their source and their end. By its fruit, the intellect awakens to recognize good and evil, light and shadow, matter and spirit; and the soul receives its office as mediator, reading the hidden currents within form and ordering its steps toward the Origin.

The Tree of Life bears a higher mystery. If the Tree of Knowledge discloses the structure of created polarity, the Tree of Life confers what stands above all polarity: union beyond division and immortality understood as uncreated participation in the One. Its fruit is the radiance of the Pleroma made manifest; it crowns knowledge with the return to that from which all proceeds and seals intelligence with communion, so that knowing is completed in being.

On the Origin of the World bears witness to the Demiurge's concealed dread: "He placed him in paradise… but the tree of life he hid, for he does not want Adam to eat from it and be immortal" (On the Origin of the World, NH II,5 lines 117.10–20, Meyer 2009). Yaldabaoth, blind and deficient, hid the Tree of Life in fear, recognizing that whoever eats becomes incorruptible and slips free of the cycles of birth, death, ignorance, and law. Such a soul ascends as one awakened to divine likeness, clothed in the radiance of the Aeons and no longer subject to the governance of the rulers of shadow.

A deeper cosmological principle appears: the Tree of Knowledge is a tempered reflection of the Tree of Life.

Knowledge proceeds from Life and, in descent, accepts veiling; radiance diminishes as it crosses the thresholds of creation, though the seal of origin remains. The two trees do not stand as adversaries; they are ordered in sacred sequence. Knowledge initiates the road of awakening; Life brings it to fulfillment. The Tree of Knowledge discloses the fragmentation of Light within form and trains the conscience; the Tree of Life restores that Light in fullness and perfects the person in communion.

A long misunderstanding has obscured this truth. In rabbinic Kabbalah, the glyph called the Etz Chaim is widely revered as a map of the divine emanations. The structured figure, admirable in symmetry and sequence, serves with profit as an image of ordered knowledge, yet it remains a figure of polarity, hierarchy, and law. Its pillars divide, its pathways discern, and its energies are weighed between mercy and severity, form and force. Such an order reflects the domain of Da'ath (knowledge) poised as a hidden bridge between the lower sefirot and the crown. The true Tree of Life exceeds diagram and measure; the glyph instructs the mind within time, but Life itself belongs to the silence of the Aeons.

The Tree of Life is apophatic, a reality beyond representation, whose fruit is tasted in contemplative stillness. It proceeds from silence rather than structure and communicates by divine eros rather than command. It is the unfolding presence of the Aeons Zoe (Life) and Phos (Light), whose union yields immortality and uncreated radiance. No pen can trace it and no sphere can divide it; it is the Aeonic procession of pure being, the unspoken Name blossoming within the soul. Most truly, it is named by silence.

If the soul confines itself to the Tree of Knowledge, beholding only duality and remaining bound within moral polarity, it abides beneath the demiurgic order. Knowledge awakens and opens a threshold; Life carries the pilgrim through. The Tree of Life grants participation in God, and participation transfigures what proposition can only indicate; by gnosis, the seeker rises through discernment, and by love, the seeker passes beyond the forms that once instructed him, keeping the truth those forms conveyed while entering the communion to which they pointed.

Christ, the Logos incarnate, fulfills both mysteries. In His teaching, He imparts the gnosis of discernment and trains the conscience to make straight judgments; in His body and blood, He offers the uncreated Life of the Pleroma, communicating what lies beyond distinction. He stands as the Tree of Knowledge in truth, awakening the mind, and as the Tree of Life in fullness, unveiling union. In Him, knowledge and life are reconciled, polarity is transfigured, and the soul is raised from remembrance into radiant unity.

Therefore, the two trees abide as sacraments of the cosmic path. The Tree of Knowledge unveils Light within matter and entrusts the intellect with judgment; the Tree of Life restores Light to its Source and perfects judgment in love. Together, they disclose the way of Theosis that begins with awakened discernment and finds perfection in the stillness of union. Knowledge that refuses charity prolongs fragmentation; knowledge ripened into love becomes life eternal, the radiant return into the uncreated bosom of the Father.

Kabbalistic and Tantric Parallels

The two trees of Eden, the Tree of Knowledge manifesting polarity and the Tree of Life perfecting union, disclose their living image within the temple of the soul. Da'ath stands as the microcosmic Tree planted in the subtle body, bridging knowledge and life; Kundalini appears as serpent fire rising through this hidden gate, awakening Neshamah to remembrance and leading Shekinah to her rest in the Holy One.

In Kabbalistic wisdom, Da'ath is named the hidden sefirah, a secret depth of knowing that unites what is below with the transcendent unity above. As the Zohar teaches, "Da'ath is the hidden sefirah, the knowledge that unites all above with all below, as sexual union unites male and female" (Zohar II:121b; Matt, Pritzker ed.). Da'ath is unveiled perception rather than bare intellection; it binds the divided into communion and opens the gate by which the soul passes from multiplicity into participation in the One, a silent bridge between Logos and Sophia, between Light that descends and Life that returns.

This hidden sefirah is figured by the serpent, for the serpent coils upon the Tree as the current of secret wisdom, drawing earth toward heaven within the architecture of creation. The serpent serves as an icon of spiral recurrence and ascending return; it moves as time turns, circling back upon its fountain. In Kabbalah, the serpent signifies Shekinah in exile, the feminine presence of Divinity abiding in matter, veiled within sexual and vital energies and hastening toward reunion with the Holy One enthroned in Keter. The same sign intimates the stirring of Neshamah, the breath-soul of divine intellect, which through Da'ath begins to perceive the unity of the emanations and the radiance concealed within every veil.

Tantric science names this mystery Kundalinī, the serpent power coiled at the base of the spine, dormant until awakened through discipline, remembrance, and holy eros. When aroused, Kundalinī ascends the central channel, illumining the centers, dissolving ignorance, and uniting Śakti with Śiva at the crown. Thus, the Śiva Saṁhitā bears witness: "As the union of man and woman is the source of creation, so the awakening of Kundalinī is the source of liberation" (Śiva Saṁhitā 5.66). Liberation here signifies the illumination of flesh and the elevation of matter into transparency before Light.

Herein, a single doctrine stands unveiled in two tongues: sexual energy is serpent energy; Shekinah, clothed in flesh, descends as dimmed brilliance; and Kundalinī is that same Shekinah returning in radiant ascent to the embrace of the Holy One beyond form and distinction. Neshamah awakens in this rising, for as Shekinah passes through Da'ath, the mind is illumined by remembrance, and the faculties of perception are transfigured into contemplation.

Da'ath is therefore the hidden Tree within. It spans the gnosis of polarity granted by the Tree of Knowledge and the unitive splendor of the Tree of Life. The serpent, rightly discerned, serves as a liberating current; Kundalinī signifies Shekinah ascending in sanctified return. Sexual energy, serpent energy, and the gnosis of Da'ath converge within the human temple to reveal embodiment as a ladder of Light that bears the pilgrim from division to union and from exile to divine rest.

Discernment remains necessary, for Light descending into matter admits counterfeit. An idol of the serpent mimics the sign and excites desire without direction, appetite without remembrance, and motion without ascent. It agitates the senses and leaves the soul unawakened; it speaks of freedom and binds the will to delusion. True serpent wisdom inclines upward with chaste hunger for the Source; the false current coils downward in addiction and forgetfulness. The wise heart distinguishes the ray that returns from the glare that consumes.

The Aeonic pattern confirms this judgment in the dual movement of Phos and Zoe (Light and Life), distinct in role and one in essence. According to the teaching of the Mystical Order of the Nazarene, the female Aeons echo one another as do the male; Zoe, fullness returning, stands as the feminine counterpart to Phos, the illuminating Logos in descent. These are personal emanations of the divine will, copies without divergence, distinguished by function and radiance within the paradox wherein the many remain the One present in each.

The Logos brings this ascent to fulfillment. As Kundalinī climbs the inner tree to unite heaven and earth within the person, so Christ ascends the Cross, the outer Tree of the world, and transfigures suffering into glory, gathering all things into Himself. The Cross becomes the raised spine of the cosmos, the axis where desire becomes liturgy and sorrow becomes illumination; there the ancient serpent is answered by the Word made flesh, and the flame once feared as passion becomes the fire of return.

Thus, Kabbalah and Tantra, received with sobriety, witness one truth: within flesh abides the hidden radiance of the Unseen God, awaiting awakening through knowledge, discipline, and love. The serpent names the current of ascent; Da'ath marks the gate of remembrance; Shekinah abides as Light in exile; Neshamah is intellect made luminous by gnosis; Kundalinī gathers what was scattered and rises toward the silent crown above all heavens. In the body, the Aeons make their appeal; in the soul, the hidden Tree unfolds; and at the threshold of praise, the way is set toward the First Gate, where doxology opens the path to Life.

The Tree as the First Gate

The Tree of Knowledge stands as the appointed gate by which humanity first entered conscious remembrance; it marked the soul's passage from unreflective innocence into the sacred burden of discernment. The interdiction of Yaldabaoth concerning its fruit established a counterfeit innocence grounded in ignorance and confined the creature to forgetfulness of origin, purpose, and destiny.

This tree was planted with providential intention to awaken the intellect within flesh, that humanity might bear the likeness of God through judgment in the light of truth. Purity without illumination remains an unmoving condition incapable of praise or sacrifice; the Tree of Knowledge roused the mind to see, to weigh, to name, and through naming to remember.

It is written, "He that hath an ear, let him hear what the Spirit saith unto the churches; To him that overcometh will I give to eat of the tree of life, which is in the midst of the paradise of God." (Revelation 2:7). The sequence stands revealed: first the Tree of Knowledge, which bestows gnosis within the experience of polarity; then the Tree of Life, which brings that gnosis to rest in the silent union of Theosis.

Knowledge awakens the exile; Life restores the homeland. One unveils the veil; the other draws the soul through.

The Tree of Knowledge administers the first sacrament: remembrance awakened within embodiment. It appoints the mind as the lamp of the body and discloses moral polarity as the living field where discernment matures into wisdom. Gnosis is beginning rather than an end. The crown of the journey is union; reintegration exceeds differentiation; the eye trained to see is perfected by becoming one with the Light that sees.

The Tree of Life remains hidden by the Archons because its fruit dissolves dominion. It confers immortality as participation rather than duration, timeless being rather than endless time; the one who partakes enters again the uncreated rest of the Pleroma. Its radiance stills the cycles of fear, judgment, and death by which the false ruler sustains his governance; and the soul that eats is released from rivalry within duality by remembrance of the ineffable Silence in which contraries are gathered without contention and rest itself becomes worship.

This path is inscribed in the human form, for the trees of Eden are mirrored within the inner temple. The Tree of Knowledge appears as the awakened mind, the rising flame of gnosis at the foundation of being; the Tree of Life appears as the transmuted light that crowns the soul in communion. Sexual energy, rightly ordered, becomes a ladder of ascent; gnosis, sanctified by love, becomes a bridge from exile into glory. A later witness has said, with partial insight and beneath the rule of the Logos, "Sexual energy is the power of the Holy Spirit; its transmutation into light ignites the serpentine fire of our inner Christ." This testimony serves as a secondary witness when read under Christ's dominion and the discipline of holy wisdom.

The two trees attain their fulfillment in Christ, in whom both mysteries converge. In His teaching, He manifests the Tree of Knowledge, awakening the hearts of the exiled to remembrance; in His body and blood, He communicates the Tree of Life, offering the fruit of unending union to those who pass with Him beyond the veil. He is the Word who awakens and the Life who restores; in Him the mind is instructed and the heart is perfected, and Beauty shines forth where judgment and charity are made one.

The Aeonic orders echo this double mystery. As the male Aeons mirror the Logos in radiance and the female Aeons echo Sophia in wisdom, so the two trees recapitulate these streams: Knowledge bearing the mark of the Logos in discernment, and Life bearing the plenitude of Sophia in communion. According to the teaching preserved among us, these Aeons abide in paradoxical unity rather than rivalry. Every Logos is the one Logos, and every Sophia the one Sophia; the Pleroma manifests multiplicity without division and unity without loss, for the One remains whole within the many and the many subsist within the One.

Hence, the Tree of Knowledge opens the first gate, the gate of awakening. Through it, humanity receives the priestly vocation, mediating between Light and density and transmuting exile into return. The Tree of Life stands before us still, hidden not by distance but by depth, dwelling in the stillness beyond emanation, and waiting to be found where Logos and Sophia converge in the soul made whole.

The fruit was tasted, and the way was opened. What remains is the pilgrimage of each soul: to awaken through knowledge, to ascend through love, and to be crowned in union by tasting immortality in the paradise of God. Beyond the beginning lies the End that is also Beginning; the soul that remembers abides without end in the uncreated Silence wherein all trees were planted before the world began.

Having traversed the first gate, knowledge is healed of pride and ordered to Beauty, and Beauty (Tiphareth) stands in the middle as the harmony of awakened gnosis; we behold the Light proceeding from the Pleroma descending through the ranks of being, and what appeared as fruit in sign becomes the movement of the Word into flesh, that He might gather the scattered and open the path of remembrance.

Chapter Five

The Descent of the Soul

Under the searching measure of Geburah, which diagnoses and purifies, let it be confessed that the Light descends without diminution, and that its condescension proceeds from mercy, free of compulsion. As the soul, by forgetfulness, passed downward through the veils and was bound to the fashions of the rulers, so the Logos, by love, traversed the same orders, clothing Himself in our condition without the stain of our confusion, that in Him the fallen course should be reversed by righteous strength.

Humanity is the Anthropos: a luminous procession from the Pleroma, wherein the Aeons abide in immutable radiance and unbroken union. From the embrace of the primal syzygies, the masculine and the feminine, whose echoes resound through all creation, each soul was brought forth as a living ray of the Unbegotten. In MON/HRC understanding, these Aeons stand as dynamic mirrors of one another, each male Aeon bearing the imprint of the Logos, each female Aeon manifesting Sophia, Zoe, and every maternal archetype, all united in paradoxical distinction.

The Anthropos descends through the Aeonic orders bearing a covenant decreed in Silence: to embody hidden Light, to awaken remembrance in the depths of matter, and to redeem the sparks scattered in the shadow of deficiency. This descent signifies vocation rather than lapse; it is a priestly ordinance before time, appointing the Pneumatics to mediation between the realms and summoning them to the fair pattern already contemplated in Tiphareth's Beauty.

As the soul traverses the Principle of Diminishing Light, each veil confers deeper concealment, moderating the brilliance while preparing the vessel for the work of restoration. Light that enters shadow remains undiminished according to essence, being tempered into a flame capable of kindling within worlds that cannot yet bear the unveiled splendor of the Pleroma. Hence, the paradox of descent: distance from the Source increases penetration into the darkness appointed for healing.

Clothed in flesh, humanity walks the earth as a living procession of the Pleroma. Though confined to the rhythms of matter, each soul bears the uncreated memory of its eternal home, a silent attraction to the One who sent it forth. Embodiment serves revelation, filling the worlds of form with the knowledge of their origin, until the Light that has descended ascends again, unveiled before the Silent Father in the fullness of Theosis.

Thus begins the destiny of mankind, the journey of Light into shadow, assured by mystery that what has been clothed shall be unclothed and what has gone forth shall return; therefore, let the Anthropos be contemplated as exemplar and measure of this descent, whose exposition now follows.

The Anthropos: Humanity as Primordial Archetype

Before the foundations of matter were established, before temporal succession stood over the eternal Light, there abided within the Silent Fullness the Anthropos, the Primordial Humanity, emanated as the first image of the Invisible Father. In the stillness before all worlds, when the Aeons contemplated the depth of their Source in perfect union, the unspoken will of the Father brought forth this luminous figure as the first form in which the Infinite would be mirrored.

The Anthropos, whose name signifies humanity in its untainted estate, stands as the archetype from whom all souls receive their form, a radiant template wrought in the silence of divine contemplation before matter received its foundation. The Apocryphon of John bears witness that the First Father, ineffable and boundless, emanated this perfect image, revealing His hidden nature.

> "And a voice came forth from the exalted aeon-heaven: 'The Man exists and the Son of Man.' … the image of the Invisible One who is the Father of all … the first Man. For he revealed his likeness in a human form."
> — Apocryphon of John (NH II,1 lines 14.24–15.6, Meyer 2009)

This manifestation discloses essence rather than appearance, for the Anthropos embodies the union of Logos and Sophia, masculine and feminine potency subsisting in undivided harmony. Resplendent with the splendour of the Father, He remains beyond the Principle of Diminishing Light, abiding in immediacy to the Source and unmarked by the veils that temper all secondary emanations.

Valentinian tradition preserves this with solemn reverence, identifying the Anthropos as the collective spiritual essence of the whole of humanity abiding unfragmented in the Pleroma. Valentinus taught that before matter was framed and before the Demiurge arranged the cosmos, this archetype stood established, containing the totality of human souls as distinct participation in one Light, varied according to mode yet unified in origin and destined end.

Within the Mystical Order of the Nazarene, it is handed down that the Aeons manifest in dynamic echo, every female Aeon bearing forth the one primordial feminine and every male Aeon exhibiting the imprint of the Logos; the Anthropos contains both before they are mirrored outward into distinct Aeonic persons. Hence, Mary Magdalene and Zoe, though diverse in power and commission, share one essence; and so the Logos with the other male Aeons, for such paradox belongs to the native order of the Pleroma, as Thunder, Perfect Mind intimates, wherein identity stands at once singular and manifold without contradiction.

Each soul descending among the forms of the world carries an uncreated remembrance of this Primordial Humanity, a memory innate and inscribed within being. Though veiled by the architecture of the Archons and clothed in corporeal opacity, the imprint abides indelible; it awakens in the stillness of contemplation, in dreams whose antiquity surpasses bodily years, in longings no terrestrial image can resolve. In the Mystical Order's teaching, this motion of recollection is the stirring of the Hidden Name, uttered by the Father over each soul in the Silence before the ages, encompassing its essence, its vocation, and its promised return.

The clay-formed account conceals this deeper genesis: the body rises from the earth while the soul proceeds from the Light antecedent to every world. Genesis recounts the shaping of man from dust, and Gnostic proclamation declares that the breath vitalizing this form descends from the Fullness, a bestowal of the Anthropos' radiance into the inert work of the Archons. Therefore, humanity bears a dual lineage: a body fashioned within the reach of Yaldabaoth and a spirit proceeding from the Father above every ruler.

In the wisdom of Kabbalah, Adam Kadmon, the Primordial Man, stands as a parallel, emanating from Ein Sof as the first template of order. Yet a divergence appears: Adam Kadmon projects the Infinite's Light into structured realms and is frequently mapped upon the glyph called the Tree of Life, whereas Gnostic insight discerns that diagram to figure the Tree of Knowledge. The true Tree of Life, consonant with Anthropic reality, remains apophatic and without fixed form, transcending diagram and glyph, manifesting as the living emanation of Zoe and Phos the Aeons of Life and Light within whom all unity is gathered.

The Anthropos likewise appears at the consummation. When all things reach their term, the scattered sparks are restored, and humanity stands gathered as one body in Him. The path that commenced in descent through shadow attains its consummation with the Anthropos standing at the threshold of the Pleroma, welcoming each soul into the undiminished radiance of its Source.

Contemplation of the Anthropos is sacramental, for prayer receives Primordial Humanity as the luminous presence in whose image the soul is formed, masculine and feminine interwoven, still and radiant, silently witnessing exile and homecoming. He is both the archetype before every framing and the completion beyond every return; from Him each soul proceeds according to mode from the one Light, and unto Him each returns bearing wisdom proved in pilgrimage through shadow.

To behold the Anthropos is to remember the rule of Fullness: what proceeds from the Fullness returns to the Fullness; Light remains Light even in the depth of embodiment; and the Hidden Name uttered in Silence shall be heard anew when the soul stands unveiled in the eternal embrace of the Father. Therefore, let the mind be set in readiness to trace the ordered procession of the descent through the Aeonic layers, which now comes to be declared in what follows.

The Descent Through Aeonic Layers

The journey of the soul from the Silent Fullness into the veiled regions of matter stands as a solemn procession through ordered Aeonic hierarchies. Each soul, begotten in the bosom of the Invisible Father, proceeds outward in radiant course, passing through the orders of Light that issue from the Pleroma, until it is clothed with the opacity of corporeal existence. This order follows the Principle of Diminishing Light: the same uncreated brilliance is received at every stage yet manifested according to mode and measure proper to the recipient, so that veils are added and gifts are conferred on for service below.

The Apocryphon of John teaches that the Aeons are eternal emanations of the Invisible One, each a distinct effulgence of divine perfection (Apocryphon of John, NH II,1; Meyer 2009). The Light remains unchangeable at the Source, while each Aeon, according to its constitution, exhibits the one Light under determinate form. As the soul proceeds from immediacy to remote orders, vision is moderated by the fitness and function of each realm; the essence abides simple and undivided while reception varies by capacity. Hence the Tripartite Tractate: "The farther away the Aeons are from the One who exists, the weaker is the power in them. Their Light diminishes in measure as they distance themselves" (Tripartite Tractate, NH I,5 lines 60.1–10, Meyer 2009). This is concealment by emanational tempering, not corruption of essence.

In the Mystical Order of the Nazarene, the path is traced through the syzygies of the Aeons, each bestowing a charism that becomes a veil when neglected. First stand Logos and Sophia, whose union generates the human soul as bearer of wisdom and seal of the living Word. Sophia ordains illumination for creation through embodied Light, while Logos inscribes within the soul the unspoken Name appointed to awaken remembrance in its hour. From this origin, the soul proceeds through Harmonia, wherein proportion and rhythm are woven into nature for discerning concord and dissonance. In Dynamis, potency of will is imparted for action among the lower realms, and the same gift, when severed from wisdom, inclines toward domination and misuse.

With further procession, the traveler enters the outer Aeons where radiance lies heavily veiled, and at last stands beneath the counterfeit heavens erected by the Archons. Hypostasis of the Archons records their counsel: "Come, let us create a man according to the image of God … that his image may become a light for us" (Hypostasis of the Archons, NH II,4 lines 89.10–20, Meyer 2009). The rulers strive to fashion a body apt for their dominion, binding perception to the courses of desire, fear, and unknowing; yet the covenant of origin abides concealed within, and no Archon effaces the seal of the Unbegotten.

The procession of descent advances by covenantal incarnation. Sophia guides gently, clothing the soul with wisdom suited to each realm, that endurance might be strengthened and understanding matured within density; Logos secures the path of return as an interior ordinance, engraving remembrance within the mind. Thus, the descent itself inaugurates the Great Work, for every charism conferred in the heights, when recalled and rightly ordered, becomes a key appointed for the gates of ascent and a remedy for faculties wounded in the shadows.

This sacrament of order shines supremely in the Economy of Christ: "Who, being in the form of God, thought it not robbery to be equal with God: But made himself of no reputation, and took upon him the form of a servant, and was made in the likeness of men: And being found in fashion as a man, he humbled himself, and became obedient unto death, even the death of the cross." (Philippians 2:6–8). The Only Begotten traverses the same orders without forgetfulness; his kenosis establishes the universal pattern by which veils become instruments of manifestation, and the road of descent is revealed as the ladder of return. What the soul bears as burden, he receives as ministry; what the realms administer as concealment, he makes serve illumination.

Kabbalistic wisdom contemplates a cognate procession from Kether to Malkuth, wherein each sefirah invests the one Light with qualities meet for creative governance. In Malkuth, the Light stands present yet clothed for the sake of the lowly, and the ascent of the soul retraces the very gates of its setting forth. The Neshamah bears the impress of the Anthropos above; the awakened Ruach becomes a ladder whereby Shekinah is exalted beside the Holy One. Such correspondences, received with reverence, confirm the law of procession and return.

A later esoteric witness speaks similarly. In the MON tradition, the very layers that once obscured the soul become stations of ascent when transfigured by remembrance, for what proceeds from Fullness returns to Fullness bearing wisdom won through faithful pilgrimage. The gifts of the Aeons, once occasions of forgetfulness, are restored as instruments of praise; the same orders that tempered the ray become causes of increase, until the interior Name is heard with clarity and the heart is conformed to peace.

Therefore, the human form, though fashioned under lesser powers, is appointed as a temple for restoration. Within this frame, the hidden flame of the Unbegotten abides; and the traveler, having learned the names of the gates, turns toward ascent vested no longer in veils but in purity fitted to behold the Father. The order of the descent disposes the mysteries of embodiment; and what follows will set forth how the body raised under the rulers is constituted as the fleshly temple, that its architecture and consecration may be rightly discerned.

Formation by Yaldabaoth and the Fleshly Temple

Within the veiled architecture of the lower heavens, Yaldabaoth, the blind craftsman and architect of illusion, undertook the shaping of humanity's corporeal vessel. His work proceeded in deficiency and by imitation, for he labored without remembrance of the Silent Source, and his hands, moving within borrowed patterns, framed the outward structure of the fleshly temple according to a wisdom shadowed by distance from the Fullness. Proclaiming himself sole god and creator, he wrought a figure bearing features learned from reflections rather than from the archetype.

The Apocryphon of John bears solemn witness to this formation and sets forth the limit of Archonic power: "Then the authorities called together all the angels and all the demons, and they took dust from the earth and formed their man. They made his body like their body, and his likeness like the image of God they had seen in the vision that appeared to them in the waters. But they did not have the power to give life to him." (Apocryphon of John, NH II,1 lines 20–30, Meyer 2009)

From this testimony, it is understood that Yaldabaoth and his companions, perceiving only distorted images, fashioned the human body as an image of their own order and as an imitation of the Image they dimly beheld. The result was a frame suitable for governance according to their measure, capable of bearing a higher presence yet unendowed with that presence while it remained under their hand. The structure stood complete in its members and joints, yet the interior was unlit, a sanctuary raised without a lamp or priestly fire.

Hence, the first state of the body: formed and articulated, yet unanimated by the power that originates in the Pleroma. Yaldabaoth shaped the frame, but the impartation of Spirit lay beyond his capacity, since his own being arose from deficiency and carried no fountain of life. Therefore, the figure reclined upon the earth, silent and without motion, awaiting consecration from a higher source.

Scripture echoes the same mystery in the primordial narrative: "And the LORD God formed man of the dust of the ground, and breathed into his nostrils the breath of life; and man became a living soul" (Genesis 2:7). The dust prepared the matter; the shaping gave the form; the breath conferred the soul's vitality. Gnostic proclamation unveils the inner economy of this act: Sophia, regarding the work framed in ignorance, moved in compassion and ordained the implanting of a spark from the Fullness, so that the vessel would receive a life suited to bear remembrance (Apocryphon of John, NH II,1; Meyer 2009). What was crafted by the craftsman according to image became apt for indwelling when the mercy of Wisdom established a principle beyond his ordinance.

Thus, the human form exhibits a twofold constitution: construction from dust under the administration of the rulers, and consecration by the descent of Light proceeding from the Pleroma. The body stands as a temple shaped within the domain of Archonic jurisdiction and, by divine philanthropy, fitted for an uncreated Flame. In this union of making and hallowing, the architecture destined for subjection is established as a site for restoration, since the same walls that circumscribe the senses are appointed to shelter the mystery of indwelling Light.

The Hypostasis of the Archons further attests to this measure and its insufficiency: "And he breathed into his face, and the man came to have a soul and remained upon the ground many days. But they could not make him rise because they lacked the power of the Spirit, which would give him the power to stand" (Hypostasis of the Archons, NH II,4 lines 91.30–92.5, Meyer 2009; cf. Genesis 2:7). Here, the boundary is made explicit: formation without Spirit does not establish the standing of the man. Accordingly, Sophia extends her beneficence, and the Logos bestows the ordinance of uprightness; animation becomes more than motion, for it is remembrance quickened, and the temple receives an inhabitant who teaches it to serve.

In the Mystical Order of the Nazarene, it is handed down that the body, though shaped under Yaldabaoth, serves the covenant of descent and return. Wisdom beheld an empty throne prepared for the lesser powers and deposited within it a luminous seed by which thralldom is translated into pilgrimage and ignorance is tutored into knowledge. The flesh thereby receives a ministry: to house the Flame that does not originate from the rulers and to become an instrument for the undoing of their false dominion through the awakening of the Name.

Hence, embodiment stands in dignity as sacred architecture woven even through ignorance, so that Light might touch all orders of creation. The form fashioned from earth is honored as a temple when Shekinah, the indwelling radiance, takes her place; and the consecration abides secure, for what Wisdom implants the rulers cannot claim, and what the Logos consecrates remains unassailable to the illusions of deficient dominion. The vessel is prepared for service when the inner lamp is kindled, and its members, once organized for rule from without, are trained for obedience to the Light within.

Apostolic admonition confirms the doctrine: "Know ye not that your body is the temple of the Holy Spirit, which is in you, which ye have of God?" (1 Corinthians 6:19). The temple designation is neither metaphor nor license for neglect; it is the charter of sanctity whereby the human frame receives a priestly vocation. The outer stone is of earth; the inner sanctuary is appointed for the uncreated Fire; and the man who understands this ordinance learns to minister at his own altar, ordering his faculties according to the Light that has taken residence.

The account of formation is rightly interpreted as the prothesis of consecration. The rulers supply the frame according to their measure, and the Father, through Sophia and the Logos, establishes the indwelling by which the frame becomes a habitation. The mystery of construction and hallowing thus prepares the doctrine that follows, how the Shekinah and the Logos are implanted within humanity as principle and end, so that the temple once raised under the lesser powers may fulfill its purpose in the Great Work of remembrance and return.

Implanting Shekinah and Logos in Humanity

Within the veiled architecture of the soul, there abides a mystery older than the world, for two seeds of divinity were implanted by the mercy of Sophia and by the radiance of the Logos. From the Silent Fullness, before the weaving of time, these seeds were entrusted to the Anthropos, that humanity might advance from bare animation unto a living temple wherein the Eternal indwells. These two are Shekinah and Logos: the hidden feminine Light and the manifest masculine Word, the one abiding as immanent compassion, the other shining forth as intelligible illumination. Their conjunction within the soul is the seal of inheritance, appointing the creature fashioned in deficiency to pass through the veils of the rulers and to return to its Source.

Shekinah is the indwelling flame, the feminine Pneuma, the radiant compassion of Sophia present within the soul. When Wisdom beheld the veil of ignorance spread over the cosmos by the blind craftsman, she clothed every soul with a spark of her hidden Light, establishing a bond which exile cannot dissolve. Hence, the Pistis Sophia testifies: "She is the Light-stream that flows into all the world of men, that it may be guided unto the Light of Lights" (Pistis Sophia, ch. 32, MacDermot 1978). The same covenant is confessed in the Zohar: "The Shekinah never departs from her children, even when they are exiled, for she is their mother in the darkness as in the Light" (Zohar I:149b; Matt, Pritzker ed.). Shekinah therefore stands as the silent mother of souls, witnessing through the ages, consoling in obscurity, nurturing the spark until remembrance flowers; veiled yet radiant, interior and unceasing in mercy. A later mystical voice echoes this interior lamp: Karl von Eckartshausen, speaking of the soul's sanctuary, declares, "The divine Light abides within all, though veiled by shadows of unknowing, awaiting the dawn of wisdom when the heart turns inward and perceives the lamp ever burning upon the altar of the soul." (Eckartshausen, Cloud upon the Sanctuary). Such testimony, though historical and beyond apostolic witness, accords with the doctrine that the hidden Light abides and awaits awakening.

To Shekinah is joined Logos, the masculine Light of intelligibility, the eternal Word implanted as the ordering principle of life and thought. The Gospel proclaims: "That was the true Light, which lighteth every man that cometh into the world." (John 1:9). The Logos is the Word through whom all things were made (John 1:3), the One who harmonizes contraries and calls the mind from shadow to knowledge of the Source. The Gospel of Philip declares: "Light and darkness, life and death, right and left, are brothers of one another ... but the Logos is the one who brings them into harmony" (Gospel of Philip, NH II,3 lines 67.25–30, Meyer 2009). A witness from outside our household acknowledges the same diffusion of the Word's life: Annie Besant observes, "He is the Life of all that is, the Self of the universe, and thus is in everything; nothing can exist apart from Him, for all existence is the flowing out into forms of His life." (Besant, Esoteric Christianity). Such recognition, though distant from our mystery, confesses participation: no creature subsists except by the Logos who confers order and being. Therefore, the Logos within is not a human faculty devised by reason; he is the uncreated Word, the Aeonic measure of concord, knitting the fragments of embodied existence into the pattern of Sophia's wisdom and supplying the very intelligibility by which discernment, integration, and ascent proceed.

A likeness of this mystery is contemplated in the Kabbalistic tree: Shekinah corresponds to Malkuth as hidden radiance in the depths of creation, while Logos appears at the heart as Tiphareth, beauty and proportion. Their mutual procession, ascending and descending through the gates, finds its rest in Kether, the silent crown beyond form. So also, within the soul, the secret flame proceeding from below and the radiant Word descending from above converge, and the human spirit becomes a living Tree of Life, rooted in earth and bearing the fruits of knowledge toward the Infinite.

In the Mystical Order of the Nazarene, this doctrine is handed down as the twin implantation of Pneuma: Shekinah as the silent flame of Sophia and Logos as the radiant Word of the Father. Shekinah remains the inner lamp that cannot be extinguished; Logos is the proclaimed Word who gathers the powers of the mind into unitive stillness. They stand as the two pillars within the sanctuary of the soul, Jachin and Boaz, between which Raguel, minister of our order, conducts the faithful into the temple not made with hands. Thus, the soul discloses itself as a microcosmic Pleroma, bearing within its center the syzygy of Sophia and Logos, the eleventh pair sealed in the Anthropos as pledge of return.

Hence, the dignity of humanity arises from this dual inheritance: Shekinah, the hidden flame of Wisdom, and Logos, the uncreated Word of the Father, inscribed upon each soul before the ages, feminine radiance and masculine wisdom united in sacred quietude. To behold oneself according to truth is to recognize the indwelling Shekinah, compassion sustaining the pilgrim, and the illumining Logos, order amid confusion. This conjunction constitutes the mystery of Theosis: Shekinah nourishes holy desire; Logos opens the path of recognition; together they awaken latent potency until the seeds entrusted by the Fullness shine as uncreated Light, no longer concealed as capacity but manifest as glory.

The human temple, framed in weakness, stands for transfiguration and bears steady witness that what proceeds from the Pleroma returns to the Pleroma. Because these indwelling gifts summon remembrance and dispose of the will for return, the Purpose of Descent, which now follows, will declare how the soul, tutored by Shekinah and ordered by the Logos, fulfills its ascent through obedient memory and the discipline of love.

Purpose of Descent is Remembrance and Return

The descent of the soul into the veiled realms of embodiment constitutes the solemn fulfillment of the hidden covenant ordained within the Pleroma before the foundations of the ages. Each soul proceeds from the Silent Fullness bearing a mission rooted in eternal intention: to extend the radiance of the Uncreated into shadowed domains, to manifest wisdom in created form, and to transfigure knowing into Theosis through the pilgrimage of embodiment.

The Gospel of Truth proclaims with solemn witness, "He became the fruit of the knowledge of the Father" (Gospel of Truth, NH I,3 lines 32.25–30, Meyer 2009). In this mystery, Christ appears as the One who descends bearing the hidden knowledge of the Father and manifests Himself as fruit offered for remembrance and restoration. His descent unveils the archetypal pattern entrusted to every soul: to proceed as seed of divine knowledge, to be sown according to ordinance within temporal order, to ripen in wisdom through trial, and to be presented at last as offering before the Silent Source.

The hymn of Paul declares of the Logos, "But made himself of no reputation, and took upon him the form of a servant, and was made in the likeness of men:" (Philippians 2:7). Here the universal canon is made manifest: kenosis is the mode by which the hidden radiance is borne in flesh, limitation is assumed as vessel for charity, and the generosity of the Eternal shines within exile. In self-emptying, the splendour of the Pleroma comes to visibility beneath the veils of creation; the same ordinance that marks the Only Begotten becomes the path of those who conformed to Him.

The Mystical Order of the Nazarene hands down that Sophia ordains this descent in wisdom. Light abiding solely within Fullness remains unmanifest; Light entering the crucible of embodiment is perfected through love. Therefore, Wisdom clothes each soul with Shekinah, the hidden flame preserving remembrance within shadows, while the Logos implants the uncreated seed of gnosis, guiding the mind toward its Origin. Descent thus discloses latent endowment, forms the virtues by deed, and bends knowledge toward perfection in the act of return.

The Tripartite Tractate confirms this hidden ordination: "For what exists within the Pleroma was needed to be revealed, that it might become perfect in knowledge and repose in its origin" (Tripartite Tractate, NH I,5 lines 57.1–10, Meyer 2009). The manifestation of Light in form serves the completion of divine knowledge; the Father wills that His radiance be known throughout the emanations, and the soul's maturation participates in that plenary recognition.

So also, the Apostle testifies, "He that descended is the same also that ascended up far above all heavens, that he might fill all things." (Ephesians 4:10). Descent functions as the condition of universal fullness; what enters the lowest orders gathers all things into its ascending return, and the fullness achieved in the Head disposes the members to be filled in due measure.

Kabbalistic wisdom contemplates a parallel mystery in the doctrine of the shattered vessels: the Light descends among fractured forms to redeem the sparks scattered within matter. Each soul, bearing Shekinah and illumined by Logos, is admitted to this sacred tikkun, the gathering of brilliance into unified radiance. Sophia extends hidden compassion to shelter and collects the dispersed splendors; the Logos orders their restoration and harmonizes their ascent with the Source. Descent, therefore, stands as the mission of remembrance: the elevation of what lay concealed into unitive perfection.

The Wisdom of Solomon speaks of Sophia's very work, saying, "For she is the breath of the power of God, and a pure influence flowing from the glory of the Almighty: therefore can no defiled thing fall into her. For she is the brightness of the everlasting light, the unspotted mirror of the power of God, and the image of his goodness." (Wisdom of Solomon 7:25–26). Wisdom proceeds in mercy and mirrors radiance within creation; souls bearing her impression may recognize what is veiled and raise it into knowledge.

Thus, the path of Theosis is traced: wisdom latent remains potential; wisdom enacted and transfigured by love is perfected. The soul clothed in matter learns to embody silent knowledge through obedient deed, to manifest hidden Light through purified presence, and to refine potential into gnosis through trial. The covenant stands from the beginning: what is begotten of Light passes through shadow to be perfected in charity and returns bearing fruit as oblation before the Father of Silence.

Accordingly, every incarnation is revealed as liturgy. Joy echoes the hidden radiance; sorrow becomes the crucible of refinement; longing sounds the interior summons of return. Time receives the rites of sanctification as the soul enacts the mystery of Theosis, making visible within veiled creation what abides eternally as uncreated Light. The procession outward and the recollection inward are one economy: remembrance illuminates the path, and charity completes the course.

Therefore, the purpose of descent abides steadfast: the unveiling of the Eternal's wisdom within the worlds, the transfiguration of creation through remembrance, and the return borne with fruit ripened by love. The soul advances as a faithful steward of what was sown from the beginning and fulfills the intention planted by the Father, offering to the Silent

Fullness a radiance deepened through exile, a knowledge proved through trial, and a wisdom enlarged by embracing all that proceeds from the Eternal.

Let this doctrine now pass into discipline: for the pattern of remembrance seeks embodiment, the ordinance of charity requires rule, and the temple fashioned for indwelling demands priestly service. In what follows, the practical life of Light within flesh will be declared, that the faithful may order their members unto sacrifice, vigilance, and praise.

Practical Implications and Living as Light in Flesh

The descent of the soul into embodiment is consecration, for the traveler bears within the veils a silent certainty of origin in Light. Within the flesh, the sanctifying radiance confers brilliance upon matter and appoints clay to become a temple. Embodiment is an entrusted sanctuary in which the hidden Flame awakens form to consecrated purpose.

Hildegard of Bingen proclaims in Scivias, "The Word is living, being, spirit, all verdant greening, all creativity. This Word manifests in every creature" (Hildegard of Bingen, Scivias II.1). Hence, the Logos implanted within each soul empowers embodiment as illumination of form: the body becomes a lamp and the Logos its flame; the flesh stands as sanctuary and the Word indwelling radiance.

A later witness, Karl von Eckartshausen, affirms in The Cloud upon the Sanctuary that the holy Light inhabits the purified heart in proportion to purification. The implication is ascetical: embodiment unfolds as discipline, with patient steadfastness and quiet fidelity each day, a gradual clarity by which the interior Fire shines unhindered. Each labor renders the members transparent to the indwelling brightness and advances the mortal frame into a liturgy of divine splendour.

In the Mystical Order of the Nazarene, it is taught that Light clothed in flesh orders thought, word, and deed according to its uncreated origin. Embodiment serves as the theatre of visible gnosis. Practices are appointed as vessels of transfiguration prayer, fixing the mind in silent remembrance; breath awakening the body as a vessel of Pneuma; fasting refining desire into a steady flame; and consecrated sexuality translating dense potency into ascending brightness.

The Gospel of Philip bears a solemn rule: "When the bridal chamber is in harmony, it brings Light" (Gospel of Philip, NH II,3 lines 67.25–30, Meyer 2009). In this ordinance, the densest mystery of embodiment sexual union is received as a sacrament. When chastened by the compassion of Sophia and the wisdom of the Logos, eros serves liberty, desire is refined into fire, and union becomes a liturgy of ascent; transmutation recalls embodied Light to its eternal Source.

Kabbalistic wisdom speaks in concord, declaring the Shekinah to be "the soul of all souls, the light that dwells within all lights" (Zohar III:159a; Matt, Pritzker ed.). In every embodied soul, Shekinah abides as a silent flame sustaining presence in exile, while the Logos orders thought and harmonizes action, guiding ascent into unitive knowledge. Their union within the body mirrors the Tree of Life: Shekinah anchors as Malkuth below, the Logos shines as Tiferet above, and the lower and upper worlds are joined through the living temple of humanity.

The Pistis Sophia witnesses that Wisdom's Light, though diffused through the cosmos, remains intact within the soul's innermost chamber, awaiting purification to shine forth. Purification proceeds by consecration: each breath becomes prayer, each labor becomes offering, and each motion of desire is tempered into compassion. Embodiment proves to be the crucible wherein dormant brilliance awakens and gnosis is manifested through deed.

Origen discerns the same economy, teaching that the soul's charge is to "make the body a temple of God, that every motion and thought may be hymn, and every deed may be liturgy" (Origen, Homilies on Leviticus II). Life conducted according to this charter becomes a continuous priesthood; even the smallest act stands before the Eternal Fire as incense.

Another later testimony, Maria de Naglowska, declares in The Light of Sex that sexual potency is a light profaned by waste and perfected by consecration (de Naglowska, *The Light of Sex*). Received as a subsidiary echo, this accords with the sacramental rule that bodily force serves illumination when governed by wisdom and mercy. Sacred union then becomes the deliberate weaving of Shekinah's compassion with the Logos's ordering Word, and unitive knowledge is kindled within the embodied temple.

The Apostle exhorts: "I beseech you therefore, brethren, by the mercies of God, that ye present your bodies a living sacrifice, holy, acceptable unto God, which is your reasonable service." (Romans 12:1). The body, so offered, stands as oblation; the flesh, so ordered, stands as temple; the embodied person, so instructed, stands as a lamp of the Eternal.

Living as Light in flesh demands that each thought be measured by wisdom, each word proceed from remembrance, and each act shine with interior fire. The initiate walks as a temple incarnate: every step an offering, every breath a prayer, every chaste union a sacrament. The veils of embodiment are rendered translucent by obedience, until the flesh bears the signature of its origin and the dust of earth is illumined by the splendour of the Father's uncreated Fire.

The practical implication of descent is a rule of embodiment: sanctify every motion into prayer, establish every desire as compassion, and consecrate every union as sacrament, until the earthen temple reveals itself as a vessel of the Eternal and humanity appears transparent to the Light from which it proceeds. Let this rule dispose the mind for the concluding seal, wherein holy rigor yields to the embrace of Mercy that gathers what discipline has prepared, as the concluding section will declare.

Descent as the First Half of Theosis

The journey of the soul unfolds as a single arc of Theosis: descent and ascent, a going forth from the Silent Fullness and a return in perfected radiance. They stand as one mystery revealed in time; what proceeds as untried brilliance returns as wisdom made luminous through embodied pilgrimage.

The doctrine of Theosis declares that the soul's descent into embodiment constitutes the first half of divinizing union. Through descent, Light emanated from the Pleroma is clothed in flesh and veiled within the architectures of creation, in order to illumine even the lowest chambers with its hidden flame. Thus, descent confers a ministry: to hallow time and to make memory fruitful in charity. Sophia, in compassion, sows each soul as divine seed into the furrows of time, while the Logos orders its path, guiding thought, word, and deed into unitive remembrance.

In this economy, the cosmos itself becomes temple, the theatre of Theosis, wherein every soul is a lamp set within its sanctuary, kindled to reveal the brilliance of the Unbegotten. Each lamp is placed by providence upon its proper stand within the created order. The soul's destiny is a return that bears what has been gathered: knowledge ripened into wisdom, love refined into flame, and embodied experience transfigured into glory.

The Mystical Order of the Nazarene teaches that descent remains the hidden half of Theosis, enacted beneath the veils of flesh, and that ascent is its unveiled consummation, when the soul stands before the Father radiant with wisdom proved through embodiment. The arc persists in unity: to proceed forth as Light clothed in form, and to return as Light unbound, restored to the Silent Fullness from which it came.

Origen discerned this pattern, teaching that "the end is always like the beginning. As from God we came forth, so to

God we shall return, but enriched with the fruits of our labor" (Origen, On First Principles 1.6). Likewise, Paul testifies, "But we all, with open face beholding as in a glass the glory of the Lord, are changed into the same image from glory to glory, even as by the Spirit of the Lord." (2 Corinthians 3:18). Descent and ascent thus form a single continuum of unveiling, wherein the hidden Flame grows into manifest radiance.

Our own teaching strengthens the same conclusion: what descends ascends, and what is clothed is unveiled. The Father has ordained that His Light, once veiled, will stand again in naked brilliance before Him.

Thus, humanity fulfills its divine vocation when the spark entrusted at descent returns unveiled, bearing the wisdom it has illumined, the love it has transfigured, and the gnosis refined through its pilgrimage. Descent becomes ascent fulfilled; embodiment becomes temple transfigured; and Theosis discloses its eternal mystery: Light proceeding from Light, returning as Light perfected in silent union with the Unbegotten One.

Geburah discloses the wound, and Mercy accomplishes the cure; therefore, let the Logos incarnate and the restoration of Sophia be contemplated, wherein the cycles of return are bent upward by charity, as Chapter Six, representing Chesed, will set forth.

The Incarnation

In the mystery of Chesed (Mercy), the descent of the Logos is confessed as the archetype of restoration, ordering the wanderings of creation toward healing and return. The eternal Word, without beginning in the bosom of the Father, manifested in time as Christ for the salvation of the many, and in Him Mercy took form; Sophia's deficiency was judged and purified, and the recursion of our wanderings, once a circle of sorrow, became a pilgrimage ascending toward the Father in orderly hope. Having considered the descent of the soul from the Silent Fullness into the veiled structures of embodiment, we now contemplate the deeper mystery: the descent of the Logos Himself, whose eternal procession is both the archetype and the consummation of all emanated beings, for in His going-forth the pattern of every return is measured and confirmed as doctrine.

In the former contemplation, we beheld how each soul, though veiled beneath the Principle of Diminishing Light, yet bears within its inmost depth an uncreated memory of the Pleroma; and before such souls entered into shadow, there stood within the Aeonic order two primal mysteries from which every procession flows: Logos and Sophia. The Logos, begotten of the Father before all ages, abides as uncreated Word eternal, proceeding without change from the Unbegotten, the Son through whom the Aeons are formed and by whom they find their rest; and Sophia, the First Thought, emanates as the radiant plenitude of Wisdom, the Mother of all who become, the luminous matrix wherein the Father's intent takes form, the Womb of Light in which all patterns are gestated before their appearance within the emanated heavens and the realms beneath. Thus, the first order is outlined in peace and in fecundity, and the end returns to the beginning in wisdom.

A paradox long hidden is thereby disclosed: Sophia, Mother of all, is discerned as bound within her emanations and in need of the liberating act of the very Logos who shines from her light; and the Logos, eternally begotten and immutable in procession, enters temporality as Christ, anointed to redeem what He eternally upholds. In this unveiling, the form of our exile is shown, for the Principle of Recursion subjects souls to cycles of embodiment, binding them within the shadow until remembrance lifts them upward again; hence, Sophia's plight mirrors every soul's wandering, and the ministry of the Logos reveals the pattern of release. Therefore, the wisdom of God orders descent for the sake of ascent, and what is assumed is healed in truth.

This is the heart of Gnosis and not a conjecture of restless thought, for in Sophia's exorcism we apprehend the pattern of salvation: Light descends into matter, accepts the constraint of shadow, and by the descent of the Logos is loosed and restored to radiance. The Apostle testifies to the same travail: "For we know that the whole creation groaneth and travaileth in pain together until now." (Romans 8:22). This groaning is Sophia's voice resounding through the order of things, awaiting purification by the one who is her joy. The Logos descends while abiding in eternal perfection and, entering time, takes upon Himself the anointing of baptism; by this Christification, He enacts redemption within history. His proclamation, "The Spirit of the Lord is upon me, because he hath anointed me to preach the gospel to the poor; he hath sent me to heal the brokenhearted, to preach deliverance to the captives, and recovering of sight to the blind, to set at liberty them that are bruised," (Luke 4:18), declares the purpose of His mission: liberation of Sophia and her children from the dominion of the Archons. Thus, the purpose of divine condescension is liberty ordered toward illumination.

Accordingly, the baptism of Christ discloses an eternal mystery: the perfect Word entering temporality, the timeless Son bearing the form of a servant (Philippians 2:7–8), the radiant One descending beneath the waters of shadow in order to raise them into Light (Matthew 3:16–17). The drama of recursion descent, embodiment, and return is unveiled as a pilgrimage transfigured by the Liberator who severs the bonds of ignorance and opens the path to Pneumatic ascent. The Revelation sets forth this figure in a vision of the woman clothed with the sun, travailing in birth while the dragon rages against her (Revelation 12:1–2; 12:13–17): Sophia appears radiant yet imperiled, and her deliverance is accomplished through the power of the Son she bore. Thus, Scripture and mystery converge to confess one soteriology, and the faithful receive its pattern as sure instruction.

Therefore, this chapter declares three interwoven mysteries for the strengthening of the faithful: first, the exorcism of Sophia as the restoration of Wisdom to her splendor; second, the baptismal Christification of the Logos as the historical enactment of eternal Mercy; and third, the doctrine of recursion as the Gospel's key by which the soul learns the way of return. Christ is manifested as the Liberator of Sophia and of her progeny, and His teaching of gnosis orders the mind to the Light that He is; by His descent, every wandering Light is led back toward the uncreated repose of the Silent Fullness, and the economy of salvation stands revealed as ordered Mercy.

Logos as Preexistent Light in All Aeons

Before the veils of form enclosed creation, and before Sophia's solitary descent gave birth to deficiency, there abided within the Silent Fullness the hidden mystery of Syzygy, the sacred union of emanations wherein the infinite wisdom of the Unknowable Father is reflected in ordered pairs. Within the Pleroma, every Aeon proceeds in a concord of male and female, each twain manifesting the eternal harmony of the Fountain from whom they flowed. Among these sacred pairings, the union of Logos and Sophia shines with primordial clarity, the First Thought and the Word, Wisdom and Utterance, joined in timeless procession from the silent depths so that the pattern of all communion might be disclosed as an ordinance of the Father's peace.

The Apocryphon of John bears witness to this primal mystery, declaring:

"And the Father looked at Barbelo with pure light which encompassed her, and she conceived from him, and he begot a spark of light with a blessedness that surpasses description. But it is not possible for any to conceive of this spark of light except the First Aeon." (Apocryphon of John, NH II,1 lines 5.5–15, Meyer 2009)

Thus is revealed the archetype of Syzygies: the Father's gaze and the receptivity of First Thought bring forth the luminous Spark that sustains the Aeonic order. From this fountainhead, the harmony of male and female emanations proceeded, each union a mirror of the primordial communion of Barbelo and the Father. Yet every Aeon remains distinct from the incomprehensible Source, who abides unmingled, beyond all emanation, hidden within ineffable Silence and unapproachable Light; and in this reserve the order of all things is preserved.

Within this ordered fullness, Logos and Sophia appear as the final pair, standing nearest the border where the Pleroma opens toward the Kenoma. They are called "lowest" by divine appointment, so that through their proximity the radiance of the Pleroma may extend into the furthest veils. Logos is the archetype of masculine procession, ordering and sustaining; Sophia is the archetype of feminine emanation, luminous and generative. Together they constitute the threshold of divine outreach, the bridge by which Light is borne into the orders of formation, and by their office, the mercy of the Source is made neighbor to what lies beneath.

Hence, every masculine Aeon echoes the Logos, bearing the silent strength and the ordering power of the eternal Word; and every feminine Aeon reflects Sophia, embodying the receptive Wisdom in which all form is gestated. As Silence emanated First Thought, and First Thought brought forth the Word, so each Syzygy manifests the abiding law: the masculine as utterance and form, the feminine as thought and matrix, both abiding in indivisible concord. Thus, the Pleroma is hymned as a harmony of paired radiances, the many returning toward the One in peace.

The Gospel of Truth proclaims this hidden architecture, saying:

> "All the emanations from the Father are pleromas, and the root of all his emanations is in the one who caused them all to grow within himself. He assigned them their destinies." (Gospel of Truth, NH I,3 lines 24.1–5, Meyer 2009)

Here it is declared that while each Aeon stands in its appointed destiny, the Logos abides as preexistent Light within them all, the silent utterance before sound, the hidden ordering before form, and Sophia abides as Wisdom nourishing every feminine emanation, the luminous matrix through which destinies are shaped. In this governance, the Father's providence is confessed, and the Aeons keep their stations in tranquil obedience.

Though Logos and Sophia are lowest in placement by appointment, they are highest in function by ordinance, for in them the Father's self-contemplation is made manifest at the very threshold of emanation. Logos is the Light veiled in every word; Sophia is the Wisdom concealed in every form; together they uphold the Syzygies as crown and root of pleromatic harmony, and their eternal union serves as the mirror wherein the Fullness beholds itself even at the borders of its descent. Thus, the perimeter of glory holds the image of its center, and the procession retains the memory of its origin.

This mystery opens the path to the contemplation of the greater economy: the Logos, from His hidden presence within all Aeons, enters the veils of temporality to become the Christ; and Sophia, though attenuated through solitary yearning, remains the unshaken archetype to which every Wisdom is conformed. In the descent of the Logos, the primordial Syzygy is renewed within the silent Pleroma and within the fabric of the cosmos, so that creation remembers its origin in the bosom of the Father. Therefore, Theosis is shown as the restoration of this archetype within the soul: to mirror the Logos in becoming Christic, and to embody Sophia in becoming luminous with Wisdom, until the inner temple reveals anew the eternal Syzygy, radiant with the Light of the Silent Fullness.

Magdalene's Exorcism

If Sophia is the luminous Womb of the universe, the radiant matrix (womb) from whom the Aeons proceed, she appears within the Gospel narrative as veiled and bound, requiring exorcism, so that Wisdom's restoration may be manifested within history. The Evangelist bears witness: "And certain women, which had been healed of evil spirits and infirmities, Mary called Magdalene, out of whom went seven devils," (Luke 8:2). Tradition has often read in this line a healing of impurity or a release from affliction; beneath the letter a deeper mystery is displayed. Magdalene stands as an icon of Sophia, our Holy Wisdom, descended into the density of matter, her brightness subdued by the veils that attend every procession into the Kenoma. Her very name becomes a veil for the Mother's plight, set before our eyes in time so that the pattern of Wisdom's healing may be confessed as doctrine.

Christ Himself unveils this when He proclaims, "But wisdom is justified of all her children." (Luke 7:35). Wisdom, though veiled, is vindicated in her works and in her offspring, for the fruit discloses the root. In Mary Magdalene, Wisdom appears embodied and awaits restoration by the Logos, who is at once her eternal counterpart and the Son revealed within time; thus, the Gospel orders our contemplation toward the union by which Wisdom's brightness is re-established.

The Gnostic tradition teaches that Sophia, moved by compassion to pour her Light into the furthest realms, entered into solitary yearning apart from her Syzygy, and her outpouring became attenuated in the regions outside the Fullness. Thus, she became entangled within the deficiency of her emanations. The Apocryphon of John narrates: "And she knew that her consort had not approved, and she repented with much weeping. The whole Pleroma heard her prayer of repentance... and they praised the Invisible, Virginal Spirit for having revealed this. And He acted with benevolence toward the repentance of His daughter." (Apocryphon of John, NH II,1 lines 30–35, Meyer 2009) In this witness, Sophia's Light is shown as dimmed, not extinguished; her dispersion arises from imbalance, and her return begins in repentance answered by benevolence. The doctrine set forth is restoration from attenuation through the mercy of the Source and the office of the Logos.

Within this mystery, the necessity of the Syzygy is revealed. Wisdom, standing as Thought, finds her completion in the Word; Logos orders and gathers, Sophia conceives and nourishes; and their concord is the ordinance by which procession holds together and return is secured. Hence, her liberation arises through the Logos, who restores multiplicity to unity and heals the dispersions of the heart. The union confessed is complementary in the Aeons and economy in time, and its fruit is peace.

The seven demons of Magdalene signify the seven planetary Archons, the rulers who bind souls to astral determinism. The Hypostasis of the Archons declares: "They made a plan together and created seven powers for themselves, and the powers created for each of them six angels, until they became 365 angels. The seven powers are named after each day of the week…" (Hypostasis of the Archons, NH II,4 lines 86.26–87.6, Meyer 2009). Thus, Mary's affliction is a figure of cosmic bondage; Sophia's Light, descending through the spheres, is veiled by successive rulers; and the casting out of the demons signifies the breaking of fate's tyranny. The exorcism, therefore, becomes the Gospel's sign of a higher freedom.

Christ the Logos comes in mercy and accomplishes the liberation He proclaims: "The Spirit of the Lord is upon me, because he hath anointed me to preach the gospel to the poor; he hath sent me to heal the brokenhearted, to preach deliverance to the captives, and recovering of sight to the blind, to set at liberty them that are bruised, To preach the acceptable year of the Lord." (Luke 4:18–19). His act upon Magdalene enacts Apokatastasis, the restoration of creation to primordial harmony. As Paul testifies: "For it pleased the Father that in him should all fulness dwell; And, having made peace through the blood of his cross, by him to reconcile all things unto himself; by him, I say, whether they be things in earth, or things in heaven." (Colossians 1:19–20). The doctrine stands: reconciliation proceeds from the indwelling Fullness of the Logos and reaches even to the bonds that fetter the soul.

Only the Logos, eternally begotten without diminution, enters deficiency without loss, and by His condescension He restores Sophia's brilliance while remaining what He is. The Pistis Sophia records: "Then the First Mystery heard Pistis Sophia, and sent a great light-stream. It came down upon the darkness and made it fade away from her." (Pistis Sophia, ch. 32, MacDermot 1978). Here the synergy is disclosed: the Light sent from on high meets the yearning below, and attenuation yields to radiance. The Gospel of Philip intimates this intimacy of Wisdom and the Savior: "Wisdom, whom they call barren, is the mother of the angels. And the companion of the Savior is Mary Magdalene. But Christ loved her more than all the disciples, and used to kiss her often on her mouth." (Gospel of Philip, NH II,3 lines 63.30–64.9, Meyer 2009). The sign here is metaphysical: the kiss manifests the exchange of Light, the reunion of Word and Thought, and the restoration of Wisdom's fruitfulness. Thus, the order of communion is read as theology rather than passion.

"The true Light, which gives light to everyone, was coming into the world" (John 1:9). "If the Son sets you free, you will be free indeed" (John 8:36). These sayings bear their witness in Magdalene's history. Mary Magdalene, first to behold the risen Christ (John 20:16–18), stands as a mirror of Sophia: as Wisdom is first to receive restoration from the Logos, so Magdalene is first to see and to announce the Resurrection. The priority of her vision becomes the seal of Wisdom's vindication, and the order of grace is displayed as a pattern for all.

The paradox that Logos is both eternal Consort and temporal Son expresses the Aeonic law wherein archetypes echo across modes without confusion. What appears as Syzygy in eternity is manifested as filial redemption within time; what is one Light in the Pleroma is disclosed in ordered relations in the economy. The theological end of such disclosure is the confession of Light restoring Light and of Wisdom standing again in clarity.

Magdalene's exorcism reveals in little the greater economy: Light descends into matter and accepts the shadow for the sake of creaturely existence; the Logos enters Sophia's attenuation and liberates her; the bonds of astral fate are sundered; and the radiance of redemption suffuses the lower orders. Sophia's restoration proceeds through the descent of Love; the Logos awakens her from deficiency, purifies her entanglement, and transfigures her exile into renewed glory; and Wisdom stands unveiled in the Pleroma, radiant in the embrace of the Silent Fullness, from whom both proceed and to whom both return.

The Baptismal Christification

How did Jesus, eternally begotten as Logos, become the Christ within time? What mystery unfolded in the Jordan that transformed the timeless Word into the temporal Savior, consecrated to redeem all emanated creation?

The Evangelist proclaims: "And Jesus, when he was baptized, went up straightway out of the water: and, lo, the heavens were opened unto him, and he saw the Spirit of God descending like a dove, and lighting upon him: And lo a voice from heaven, saying, This is my beloved Son, in whom I am well pleased." (Matthew 3:16–17).

Here, the veil is lifted upon a mystery hidden since before the framing of the worlds. Though Logos is eternally begotten, perfect and immutable within the Silent Fullness, His baptism reveals His purpose. Incarnation enfleshes the Word; baptism anoints the Word as Christ within history. Logos is the eternal Word beyond time; Christ is the anointed Word within time, bearing mission and mantle in the divine economy.

The Trimorphic Protennoia unveils this aeonic descent: "I am Protennoia, the Thought that dwells in the Light. She who exists before the All. I move in every creature… I became Christ" (Trimorphic Protennoia, NH XIII,1; Meyer 2009). Protennoia, the primordial Thought, proceeds as Voice and Word, descending through every realm until manifesting as Christ within time. Thus, baptism is the historical moment where the eternal procession is sealed within matter (Matthew 3:16–17). Though eternally Light, Logos becomes Christ in the aeonic economy when anointed by the Spirit, consecrating not Himself only but creation itself for redemption.

In this act, the Logos recapitulates all aeonic descent, retracing the fall of Sophia's scattered Light, gathering her fragments into Himself. His baptism is therefore a cosmic reorientation, anointing Him to liberate Wisdom from deficiency and restore her progeny to the Pleroma.

The Gospel of Philip proclaims: "The Christ has everything in himself, whether man, angel, or mystery, and the Father" (Gospel of Philip, NH II,3; Meyer 2009). Christ thus embodies the totality of the Logos in flesh, manifest without diminution. Logos is the uncreated Word eternally begotten; Christ is the anointed Word manifested in history, crowned by the Spirit to enact the cosmic reconciliation ordained before time.

The Gospel of Truth adds: "He became a guide, quiet and in leisure. In the middle of a school, He came and spoke the word as a teacher. Those who were wise in their own estimation came to test Him, but He confounded them because they were empty" (Gospel of Truth, NH I,3; Meyer 2009). Here, the anointing is revealed in function: Christ as the teacher of gnosis, unveiling the mysteries veiled from the foundation of the world (Matthew 13:35). He is Logos eternally; baptism consecrates His public mission, and the Spirit's resting upon Him declares His authority among men (Matthew 3:16–17).

The Gospel of the Egyptians affirms: "He is the great invisible Spirit. He is the First Aeon, He the great Christ" (Gospel of the Egyptians, NH III,2; Meyer 2009). The eternal Aeon becomes manifest in time through the baptismal anointing, bridging uncreated eternity and created history in His own Person (Matthew 3:16–17).

Thus, baptism manifests the eternal Son within history. The Spirit's descent reveals His mission. The Logos, already Light of Light, receives the visible seal of the Spirit so that creation itself may behold His anointing.

John the Baptist testifies: "And I knew him not: but he that sent me to baptize with water, the same said unto me, Upon whom thou shalt see the Spirit descending, and remaining on him, the same is he which baptizeth with the Holy Ghost. And I saw, and bare record that this is the Son of God." (John 1:33–34). The baptism, therefore, unveils within the temporal order the eternal communion of Father, Son, and Spirit: the Father declares, the Spirit descends, the Son receives. The Trinity, hidden before all ages, is disclosed within time at the Jordan.

The Fathers discerned this mystery. Irenaeus declares: "He came to save all through means of Himself – all, I say, who through Him are reborn unto God: infants, and children, and youths, and old men" (Irenaeus, AH II.22.4). In baptism, the Logos consecrates all ages, all conditions, and all orders of being, drawing all into His Christic anointing. Origen likewise taught that Christ's descent into the waters sanctified all waters, making baptism a universal wellspring of rebirth.

The implication for us is profound. Just as the Logos becomes Christ through anointing, so do we, who are Logos-seeded beings, become Christic through baptism. Within us lies the implanted Word as a hidden spark; baptism ignites it into flame. The Spirit descends not merely to cleanse but to christify, awakening gnosis from potential into actuality, from concealed seed into radiant branch. Baptism thus seals us with the same anointing by which He was anointed, initiating us into the pattern of Theosis.

In the teaching of our Order and church, this is the sacramental path: the spark of Logos, dormant within, is fanned into flame by water and Spirit, uniting the initiate to the Father's embrace and to the Son's anointing. The baptized one becomes a vessel of radiance, a Christic presence within time, bearing the fragrance of redemption into the world.

Therefore, baptism is the visible seal of the cosmic economy of salvation. It is the earthly mirror of the heavenly procession: Logos descends into flesh, is anointed as Christ within time, and ascends bearing all into the bosom of the Father. So too do we, descending as sparks into matter, rise through baptismal anointing into Christification, that we may share in His mission and reflect His Light.

Thus, in the Jordan River, we behold both pattern and promise: Logos becomes Christ, that creation might become Christic. Baptism is the anointing of eternity upon time, the descent of the Spirit upon flesh, the unveiling of the hidden Word as manifest Light. And in that Light we too are called to walk, until all things are gathered again into the Silent Fullness from which they first proceeded.

The Crucifixion

When Christ descended into the waters of the Jordan, the holy warfare was inaugurated and ordered toward its consummation at Golgotha; from that font the mission went forth, and upon the Cross the victory was sealed. The one who entered was the living temple in whom the Logos, eternal and divine, made His dwelling, and the Spirit descended as clothing of Light, enveloping Jesus with the radiance of the Pleroma: "And the Holy Ghost descended in a bodily shape like a dove upon him, and a voice came from heaven, which said, Thou art my beloved Son; in thee I am well pleased" (Luke 3:22). The Gospel of Philip explains this mystery: "It is not the Light that is baptized, but the one who receives the Light" (Gospel of Philip, NH II,3; Meyer 2009). Thus, the Logos condescended, and the man Jesus was suffused with the plenitude of Wisdom, standing manifest as the Christ.

Before this anointing, Jesus stood as a sanctified vessel, sinless, righteous, and pure; by baptism, the veil between flesh and Spirit was opened, and the full agency of the divine economy operated in Him. Adam was animated by the breath of the Demiurge; Christ was filled by the Light of the Most High (Genesis 2:7). The Logos, though equal with God, emptied Himself into flesh (Philippians 2:6–8), entering weakness as mission, and this kenosis prepared the ground for the confrontation at Golgotha, where Archonic dominion would be broken.

The baptism constituted the first strike in the conflict of the ages. The Archons, blind rulers sustained by polarity and ignorance, beheld an incarnate anomaly, One in whom the indivisible Unity of God dwelt bodily. The Logos entered their domain to unseat the economy by which they enthroned themselves and to reveal the kingdom that abides.

Upon the Cross Christ accomplishes. His cry, "It is finished:" (John 19:30), marks the moment of consummation. He bore within Himself the accumulated anguish of creation, together with scourge and spear. The Apocryphon of John bears witness that the Archons fashioned humankind to serve their designs and sought nourishment in the psychic emissions of the soul in grief without healing, desire severed from charity, worship distorted by fear; such fragmentation is their harvest (Apocryphon of John, NH II,1; Meyer 2009). The Lord's passion is whole and freely embraced; charity remains indivisible; obedience stands perfect; and this integrity silences the Archonic hunger, for unity confounds powers trained only to divide.

The Apostle names the field of combat: "For we wrestle not against flesh and blood, but against principalities, against powers, against the rulers of the darkness of this world, against spiritual wickedness in high places." (Ephesians 6:12). These "high places" signify the false heavens of the Hebdomad, imitative Paradises that shimmer as reward yet bind as containment. When Christ speaks to the thief, "And Jesus said unto him, Verily I say unto thee, To day shalt thou be with me in paradise." (Luke 23:43), He addresses the upper veil of Archonic power; He enters as Lord to break its hold and to lead forth the captives.

Hence begins the victorious ascent through the tollhouses spoken of in the Pistis Sophia and in the Apocalypse of Paul. The detained are questioned there and held unless they bear gnosis and purity. The Lord carries no ignorance, no karmic debt, no forgetfulness. His entry declares judgment; His silence confounds. Each ruler meets the Light that remembers, and remembrance disarms them. Their power extends only over oblivion; confronted with perfect memory, they are undone. Therefore, the Apocalypse declares: "I am he that liveth, and was dead; and, behold, I am alive for evermore, Amen; and have the keys of hell and of death." (Revelation 1:18). The Gospel of Nicodemus recalls that the King of Glory shattered the gates of Sheol and bound its princes beneath His feet (Gospel of Nicodemus; ANF 8).

In this work, the Logos is joined by Wisdom. As He descends, Sophia summons from above. She who once scattered her Light into Adam now gathers it. She who spoke through the serpent as the Logos' veiled vessel of Wisdom, awakening gnosis, now calls the Pneumatics heavenward. "Wisdom hath builded her house, she hath hewn out her seven pillars:" (Proverbs 9:1). These pillars are the stable ordinances of ascent by which her children rise in ordered peace.

At the Cross, she is mirrored in Mary Magdalene. She stands as mourner and mystagogue, keeping sabbath in understanding. The union of Wisdom and Word is manifest as sacrament: He rends the gates; she, by faithful love, draws the souls through. Together they open Da'ath, the threshold between worlds, and the passage is altered; death's portal becomes a way of Life; the guarded road of the Archons is unveiled as remembrance; fear yields to charity, and the exiled are gathered.

This mystery is granted for enactment. "And he took bread, and gave thanks, and brake it, and gave unto them, saying, This is my body which is given for you: this do in remembrance of me." (Luke 22:19). Remembrance is more than recall; it is the gathering of what is scattered, the reintegration of the soul according to Christ's order (1 Corinthians 11:24–26). The Eucharist is therefore the Church's resonance with the Passion. Bread and wine are pledges of the Sacrifice and instruments of participation (1 Corinthians 10:16). Each true Eucharist renews the power that overthrew the Archons, kindling within the faithful the same virtue that laid bare their craft (Colossians 2:15). The Church participates in the Passion's victory, and the Mystery communicates power.

The Fathers bear witness. Melito of Sardis, preaching the Pascha, declared that "He who hung the earth in place is hanged; He who fixed the heavens in place is fixed to a tree." The paradox reveals the strength: the Infinite assumes flesh; flesh is stretched upon wood; and from the wood the grace of redemption is diffused through the cosmos. The Eucharist extends this paradox into the faithful, so that finite vessels may bear the resonance of the Infinite in humility.

Thus, the crucifixion stands as consummation rather than conclusion. Christ bears the sum of suffering as priestly oblation. The rulers approach as devourers and are confounded. Sophia lifts from above, the Logos rends from below, and the Pneumatics are called into birth between. The Cross is raised as the axis of a new creation; its wood becomes a bridge between worlds; its nails serve as the seal of reconciliation by which heaven and earth are made one.

The crucifixion is the decisive passage of the economy: division yields to unity, ignorance yields to remembrance, death yields to Life. In that hour Paradise trembles, Sheol is broken, Sophia calls, and the Logos proclaims the end accomplished "It is finished:" (John 19:30), fulfilled in truth and established forever.

The Gospel's Hidden Doctrine of Return

If the soul has descended before, the canonical Scriptures bear signs of such recursion. The sacred writings veil the mystery of return as a cyclical pilgrimage of the spirit through embodiment ordered toward final rest in the Silent Fullness, and beneath the literal sense, the doctrine of return gleams as scattered rays awaiting collection into the lamp of gnosis. Christ Himself unveils this mystery with unflinching clarity: "And if ye will receive it, this is Elias, which was for to come." (Matthew 11:14). In this word, He declares John the Baptist as the return of Elijah. Reincarnation appears here as the latent doctrine within Israel's expectation. The prophet who ascended in fire descends again, clothed in new flesh, for his mission awaited consummation, and the cycle thereby serves providence rather than caprice.

The Letter to the Hebrews deepens the mystery through Melchizedek: "Without father, without mother, without descent, having neither beginning of days, nor end of life; but made like unto the Son of God; abideth a priest continually" (Hebrews 7:3). Here, one is manifest within history and free of ordinary genealogies. His presence reveals that certain souls, fashioned for enduring ministries, appear across epochs and transcend linear birth and death. Melchizedek thus figures those set apart for the work of reconciliation, descending as needed by the will of the Father before the world's foundation, and his office displays the constancy of divine purpose.

Again, the canonical Gospel speaks with subtle clarity. The disciples ask concerning the man born blind: "And his disciples asked him, saying, Master, who did sin, this man, or his parents, that he was born blind?" (John 9:2). Their question presupposes a life known before birth. Christ directs them beyond blame to the higher cause: "Jesus answered, Neither hath this man sinned, nor his parents: but that the works of God should be made manifest in him" (John 9:3). Pre-existence is acknowledged in their understanding, and providence governs its outcome, so that embodiment becomes the stage upon which the works of God are made known, and the soul is trained in remembrance.

Even the expectation of the crowds preserves this knowledge. To John, they ask, "Art thou Elias?" (John 1:21). This inquiry arises from Israel's esoteric hope that Elijah would return before the Messiah (Malachi 4:5). The very asking discloses that the doctrine of return stood within the people's memory, guarded beneath prophetic symbols yet alive in the faithful consciousness, and thus Scripture bears the pattern in the hearts of those who waited.

The Nag Hammadi writings unveil what Scripture veils. The Hypostasis of the Archons declares that the soul descends through planetary spheres, each governed by rulers who bind it unless gnosis liberates it (Hypostasis of the Archons, NH II,4; Meyer 2009). This architecture mirrors the doctrine of recursion: each descent clothes the Light with greater opacity; each return tests the soul under Archonic dominion, until the remembrance of Christ breaks the cycle. Likewise, the Gospel of the Egyptians affirms: "They had not been completed and had not returned to the Father of the All. They will remain in the places where they were born until they complete the deficiency in themselves" (Gospel of the Egyptians, NH III,2; Meyer 2009). Here, the law of return is joined to healing; deficiency is mended by ordered passage, and the soul's integrity is restored in patience.

From this witness emerges the principle of diminishing Light. Each descent into embodiment veils the spark more deeply; each ascent without gnosis leaves remnants unhealed and thus compels return. The Archons exploit this law to bind souls within recurrence, seeking sustenance from unresolved energies. Christ fulfills the law of return and shatters the wheel. He enters the cycles by compassion, and the wandering becomes ascent; the pattern is upheld and its tyranny broken, and return is made into a ladder of remembrance.

This mystery extends to the angelic economy. In the traditions of Israel, Elijah becomes Sandalphon, the great archangel who weaves the prayers of humanity into crowns before the Throne (Chagigah). His office proceeds by consecrated recursion: prophet in flesh, then angelic minister, then herald as John before the face of the Lord. When the unborn Baptist leapt in Elizabeth's womb at Mary's greeting (Luke 1:41; Luke 1:44), Sandalphon recognized the descent of Logos–Sophia and rejoiced that his mission aligned with the advent of final redemption. Recursion thereby becomes a consecration to service, and vocation ripens across modes in obedience to the Most High.

Nor is this pattern alien to the Logos. He has descended before. In Eden, He came as the serpent, as the Logos' veiled vessel of Wisdom, awakening gnosis to Adam and Eve. That voice was compassion clothed in symbol and stirred the first emanated ones to remembrance. He descended again in manifold forms as angel, as prophet, as hidden guide until, in the fullness of time, He entered as Christ Jesus to gather the scattered sparks. The Logos thus transfigures recursion, and His repeated advents sow remembrance among the children of Sophia, so that the end answers to the beginning.

The words of Christ confirm this mystery: "Jesus said unto them, Verily, verily, I say unto you, Before Abraham was, I am." (John 8:58). He reveals eternal pre-existence and free entrance into time. His "I AM" cuts through the veil of temporality and shows that His movement within history proceeds by compassion. He returns and breaks the return, and the souls are led out of repetition into the Light that knows no descent, for His presence is the end toward which the cycles tend.

"Him that overcometh will I make a pillar in the temple of my God, and he shall go no more out: and I will write upon him the name of my God, and the name of the city of my God, which is new Jerusalem, which cometh down out of heaven from my God: and I will write upon him my new name." (Revelation 3:12). To be made a pillar is to stand immovable in the temple of the Fullness and to cease from going forth. Here, the end of the return is promised. The soul abides in unveiled radiance, and apokatastasis is confessed as restoration to the Origin, rest within Silence, and stability in Light.

The early Fathers hint at this hidden doctrine. Origen taught the pre-existence of souls, that each descends by divine justice and ascends by divine mercy until purified for union with God (Origen, On First Principles). Clement of Alexandria described human life as a school of souls, many lives allotted for the spirit's training (Clement of Alexandria). Irenaeus, guarding the Church from excess, yet proclaimed that Christ "recapitulated all things in Himself" (Irenaeus, AH). In this recapitulation the cycles are gathered to a single Head and brought to completion.

Thus, recursion appears as a providential pilgrimage. Each life is a veil and unveiling; each embodiment is a chapter in ascent. The goal is Theosis, the soul transfigured into the likeness of God. Through many lives, the spark is tempered; through Christ, the cycle receives its crown, and the divine image is restored in clarity.

For Theosis is the telos of recursion. The soul becomes a luminous temple of the Most High. Having passed through many garments, it is clothed in Light; having wandered through many worlds, it is gathered into Silence; having borne the likeness of Adam, it is crowned with the likeness of Christ and reveals within itself the union of Logos and Sophia. The doctrine thereby instructs the faithful in hope and orders desire toward the Pleroma.

Therefore, the hidden doctrine of return discloses the mercy of the Father, the compassion of Sophia, and the liberating power of Christ. The Father ordains return for healing; Sophia plants memory within each cycle to draw souls upward; Christ descends again and again to turn wandering into ascent. In Him, recursion becomes consummation, until all emanated sparks are restored to the Silent Fullness whence they first shone before the foundation of the world.

Addressing Potential Objections

Before we enter these unveiled mysteries, it is meet to address certain objections that may arise within the contemplative mind, lest subtle confusion obscure the radiant clarity of Gnosis.

Some may question how Logos, being Sophia's Son, can also be her Consort. This difficulty stems from reading Aeonic relations through the categories of material kinship rather than through emanational procession. Within the Pleroma, relations are ordered by archetypal concord; the categories of created existence, generation, marriage, and hierarchy do not govern them. Sonship signifies proceeding origin; consortship signifies ontological complementarity. Logos proceeds from Sophia as Word from Thought and abides her eternal counterpart within their Syzygy. Their union is archetypal, the harmony of utterance and matrix, activity and receptivity, within the silent embrace of the Unknowable Father. Scripture offers types of this paradox: Christ is both "I am the root and the offspring of David," (Revelation 22:16), origin and descendant in one mystery; He is the Paschal Lamb offered and the High Priest who offers (Hebrews 9:11–12). These mysteries illuminate the simultaneity of eternal relations. Thus Logos is both the Son who proceeds and the Bridegroom who embraces Sophia, and this concord is mirrored in the Eucharist, wherein bread and wine, body and spirit are present in one harmonious presence.

Others cite the verse: "And as it is appointed unto men once to die, but after this the judgment:" (Hebrews 9:27), as if it contradicted the mystery of repeated embodiment. The verse affirms that within each incarnation there is a death and a judgment. Each life bears its own reckoning and unveils the soul's progress or deficiency. Thus, the saying remains wholly true within recursion: man dies once in each embodiment, and after that comes the weighing of his gnosis and works. This judgment propels the pilgrimage onward, each life unveiling another step toward consummation in Light. As Israel passed through many stations before the Promised Land (Numbers 33), so the soul advances through many dwellings before its inheritance in the Pleroma. The verse, therefore, affirms the solemn rhythm of descent and ascent, death and judgment, until the pilgrimage is fulfilled.

Finally, some stumble at the claim that Sophia required an exorcism, inferring that she became evil. Evil pertains to willful rebellion; Sophia's state is attenuation. Her Light became entangled within her emanations, dimmed by the weight of descent into matter. The Logos' exorcism is the restoration of the loosening of her Light from its bonds, the healing of deficiency, the return of Wisdom to primordial radiance. Her history echoes the parable of the lost coin (Luke 15:8–10): she is precious though lost, and heaven rejoices when her brightness is restored. Her purification by the Logos prefigures the final apokatastasis, the restoration of every spark to its true estate.

Thus, contemplated within the silent harmonies of emanation rather than the logic of material categories, these objections are resolved; in the mysteries of Logos and Sophia, history and eternity are reconciled, and the concord of the Unbegotten Father stands revealed.

Christ as Logos Beyond Recursion

Christ is revealed as the Logos who, out of compassion, descends again and again for the salvation of Sophia and her children. From the first emanations of creation to His veiled approach in Eden, the serpent as the Logos' veiled vessel of Wisdom, awakening gnosis from His incarnation as the Word made flesh to His luminous anointing in the waters of baptism, the Logos enters creation at every stage of its wandering, bearing Light into shadow to awaken what lies veiled in deficiency. His descent is mercy, a voluntary condescension that loosens the cycles and restores order among the things below. He bears the marks of patience in every economy, and His approach is measured, healing without compulsion and summoning without coercion, so that freedom itself becomes the seal of restored order.

His baptism marks the solemn moment when the eternal Logos is manifested as the Christ within time, receiving the Spirit's anointing to initiate the cosmic redemption ordained before the foundation of the world. In that hour, the veil between eternity and time stood parted, and the One abiding unchanging within the Silent Fullness entered history as the anointed Savior. Logos is eternally the Word begotten before all worlds; in baptism, He is shown as Christ the Redeemer who enters the cycles in order to bring them to their end.

Thus He declares, "Jesus said unto them, Verily, verily, I say unto you, Before Abraham was, I am." (John 8:58), unveiling that His presence is both eternal and historical, transcendent and immanent. He abides outside all cycles and freely enters them to transfigure them into the ascent of gnosis. In Him, history ceases to be a closed circle of return and becomes a spiral pilgrimage moving toward the consummation of all things, for the First and the Last makes time itself serve salvation (Revelation 1:17; 22:13).

This spiral ascent governs the mystery of recursion. While the Archons bind souls in repetition, Christ bends the wheel upward, transforming recurrence into remembrance and remembrance into restoration. What appears as sameness is revealed in Him as gradual unveiling: each cycle a higher turn, each embodiment an opportunity for fuller awakening, until the fragments of Sophia are recollected into the bosom of the Father and the many are gathered into one peace.

The Gospel of Thomas speaks to this transfiguration of the soul's journey:

> "You have drunk, you have become intoxicated from
> the bubbling spring which I have measured out"
> (Gospel of Thomas, logion 13, Meyer 2009).

To drink of the Logos is to receive divine remembrance, a holy inebriation that dissolves forgetfulness. As wine alters sense for a time, so the wisdom of Christ reforms the soul enduringly, filling it with the sober ecstasy of Light. This intoxication stands as a sacramental reversal of ignorance: a Spirit-filled clarity by which the cycles of return are broken and the soul is reclothed in its uncreated name before God.

The baptism of the Jordan (Matthew 3:16–17), the wine of Cana (John 2:1–11), and the blood of the Eucharist (Luke 22:20; 1 Corinthians 10:16) proceed from the same bubbling spring of the Logos and pour remembrance over creation. As the disciples at Pentecost appeared drunk with new wine (Acts 2:13), so all who receive His Spirit are borne beyond the circuits of the Archons into the freedom of divine joy, for charity casts out the fear that binds (1 John 4:18).

Yet the descent of Christ is always for Sophia and for her progeny. Her scattered sparks, imprisoned in bodies and in worlds, wander through recursion until the Bridegroom gathers them. The Logos as Consort-Son enters her exile to restore, weaving the rounds of return into a greater tapestry of ascent. Sophia's children, once laboring under endless recurrence, find in Him the ladder of return, each rung illumined by His condescension and made firm by His victory.

Nor is this restoration bounded by humanity. As Paul bears witness, "For we know that the whole creation groaneth and travaileth in pain together until now." (Romans 8:22). The Logos comes to redeem souls and to liberate the cosmos from the bondage of corruption (Romans 8:21). The courses of stars and seasons and the groaning of matter under entropy find their consummation in Him who is Alpha and Omega, the beginning and the end (Revelation 22:13; Revelation 1:8); and the universe, subject to futility for a season, is prepared for the glory of its renewal (Romans 8:20; Revelation 21:5).

The doctrine of apokatastasis, universal restoration, therefore, crowns the mystery of recursion. Christ fulfills the cycles by gathering all things into their uncreated origin. As the Revelation promises:

> "Him that overcometh will I make a pillar in the temple of my God, and he shall go no more out: and I will write upon him the name of my God, and the name of the city of my God, which is new Jerusalem, which cometh down out of heaven from my God: and I will write upon him my new name." (Revelation 3:12).

Here the goings-forth cease; the pilgrim becomes a pillar, immovable within the temple of the Most High. The soul, after many wanderings, is made steadfast in Light, clothed in the raiment of eternity, and abides in the Silent Fullness. The promise extends to things visible and invisible, to powers and dominions, for in Him all things cohere and find their true boundary in love.

Thus, Christ stands beyond recursion. He is the Logos before all emanations, the First and the Last, the One who was with God and was God. He is also the compassionate Redeemer who enters time, anointed as Christ within history, to break the dominion of the Archons and to bend recurrence into ascent. In Him, the wandering becomes pilgrimage, the burden becomes liberty, and repetition finds its consummation in peace.

In Christ, the whisper once clothed in symbol becomes manifest wisdom; baptism becomes the anointing of the cosmos; recursion becomes the spiral ascent; and death becomes the portal into incorruption. He is the descent of Light into darkness, the remembrance that undoes forgetfulness, and the fulfillment of Sophia's yearning in the embrace of the Father, so that the order of love stands secure.

Therefore, the Gospel's hidden doctrine of return finds its crown in Him. Apart from Christ, recursion remains exile without end; in Christ, recursion becomes the path to Theosis, the transfiguration of the soul into divine likeness. Through Him, every emanated spark is recollected, every veil is lifted, and every cycle is brought to its ordained fulfillment, so that Wisdom's children are gathered into the repose of the Silent Fullness.

Thus, we close by confessing that Christ is within and beyond history, the Logos who enters again and again, and the Logos who ends all return. With Chesed (Mercy) accomplished in His descent, we turn to Binah (Understanding): "discernment of Archonic illusions," wherein the pilgrim learns the rule of distinction, weighs semblance against Light, and is armed for the judgments of understanding that begin the next ascent.

Chapter Seven

Escape from the Archons

In the mystery of Binah, which is Understanding, we discern how mercy descends from above to expose the illusions of the Archons and to teach the soul the difference between shadow and Light. For the heaviest yoke upon humanity abides not in the decrees of mortal despots nor in the fleeting structures of earthly empire, but in the unseen dominion of those rulers begotten of Yaldabaoth's deficiency. These wardens of the Hebdomad weave fetters of fate around the soul, persuading mortals that bondage is reality and deception divine ordinance. By fear they bind, and by forgetfulness they estrange, so that the Pneumatic spark may neglect its home in the ineffable Light and fail to ascend to the Father who is before all beginning.

Their dominion appears in diverse modes: Adonaios cloaks tyranny with the semblance of divine will; Oraios encloses the soul in fatalism, enslaving it to blind necessity; Astaphaios entices through the intoxication of flesh, drawing the heart into forgetfulness of its immortality. These counterfeit governors enact the arrogance of Yaldabaoth, who proclaimed himself sole God while remaining ignorant of the Source that transcends him.

The Apostle bears witness concerning their shadowed rule: "And having spoiled principalities and powers, he made a shew of them openly, triumphing over them in it." (Colossians 2:15). And the Gospel of Mary declares that when the soul rises steadfastly, "the Powers trembled, and they cried out, saying: 'Where are you going, destroyer of our realm?'" (Gospel of Mary, BG 8502,1; Meyer 2009).

Against this tyranny descended the Logos, clothed in frail flesh yet bearing the authority of the uncreated Pleroma. He came to reveal the Father whom the rulers cannot behold, and to rectify through Wisdom what deficiency had produced through error. For where Sophia's wound gave rise to Yaldabaoth and his ministers, the Logos by merciful condescension transfigures that wound into the doorway of healing. Through Him, the Aeons Zoe and Phos, Life and Light, shine forth as the antidote to death and ignorance.

This mystery is the true war of spirits. It is the triumph of Love which is Light, dissolving the bonds by which the Archons enslave, restoring memory of the silent covenant hidden within the Pneumatic heart, and unveiling that submission to the Father is the only freedom unassailable by rulers below. Christ's descent is therefore humanity's remembrance: that beyond the iron heavens abides the silent embrace of the Ineffable, and within every soul endures the spark which no Archon can extinguish.

The Nature of the Archons

The Archons stand as governors of the Hebdomad, begotten of Yaldabaoth's ignorance and estranged from the Fountain of Light. They hold no portion in the creative plenitude of the Father, nor do they emanate wisdom from the Aeons. Their dominion subsists parasitically, constructed upon deception, sustained by fear, and veiled against gnosis. They are jailers of mind and soul, weaving counterfeit architectures of thought and perception to ensnare the Pneumatic spark in chains of amnesia, lest it remember its uncreated origin and ascend beyond their counterfeit order.

They generate nothing from themselves but draw upon the brilliance of souls enthralled in ignorance. As usurpers fastening upon what is living, they drink the radiance of those subdued, transmuting loosh into their sustenance and fear into their draught. Thus, they erect thrones of borrowed Light, feeding upon the very sparks they conceal. For this reason, their power is fragile: when even one soul remembers, their web unravels, and their thrones dissolve as wax before flame.

Each Archon manifests the corruption of an Aeonic reality. Elaios counterfeits mercy, binding souls in false grace that excuses bondage while withholding freedom. IAO distorts purification into judgment without transformation, kindling a fire that consumes yet does not illumine. Sabaoth, before repentance, made war his law, stirring nations with conflict divorced from justice. Astaphaios seduces through sensual intoxication and spiritual amnesia, lulling the soul into forgetfulness of its immortal dignity. By these corruptions, they enthrone error, fashioning order as enslavement, destiny as fatalism, and freedom as rebellion against their false law.

Their whisperings echo in the silent chambers of the mind: "You are alone; you are unworthy; your desires define you; your weakness is your destiny." Thus, they enthrone illusions of selfhood and enthrall the heart in despair. They declare shadows to be substance and idols of smoke to be truth. Their seals mark the soul with counterfeit identity, stamping weakness as nature and despair as law. Yet their authority is void, for their decrees bear no likeness to the Father, and remembrance shatters their inscription.

So testifies the Apocryphon of John: "Their delight is in deception, and their power is in forgetfulness." (Apocryphon of John, NH II,1; Meyer 2009). And the Gospel of Truth proclaims: "Error was angry with Him when it was nullified. It did not find a path." (Gospel of Truth, NH I,3; Meyer 2009). Thus, the saints discern the economy of their reign: they subsist only where ignorance abides, and their rule endures only while the divine spark slumbers. When the soul turns in humility toward the Father, the illusion of their thrones dissolves. Resistance consists in remembrance of the covenant sealed within the Pneumatic heart. When Light is recalled, their chains stand revealed as phantasms, their kingdoms as mists without substance, and their decrees as echoes fading in silence.

Therefore, the Apostle declares: "Be not overcome of evil, but overcome evil with good." (Romans 12:21). The good that triumphs is the Light remembered, and the evil that perishes is its veiling. When the spark awakens, the Archons are starved of sustenance, their shadow-law collapses, and the soul ascends beyond their iron heavens into the Fullness of the Father. Thus, the saints behold the difference between true authority, which flows from the Father's Light, and false authority, which withers when remembrance dawns.

The Illusion of Authority

The Archons, having enthroned themselves as rulers of mind and soul, extend their dominion into the very architectures by which humanity orders its existence. Their deception does not halt at the threshold of the individual heart but seeps into religion and governance alike, warping what was meant to mirror the silent order of the Pleroma into instruments of bondage. Their counterfeit hierarchy clothes itself in semblances of majesty, though severed from the Light that alone grants authority its truth.

Religion can manifest Archonic bondage when hierarchy is estranged from the Fountain of Light and descends into legalistic domination devoid of gnosis. True hierarchy is the reflection of divine order. In distortion, the voice of Adonaios is heard, the Archon who twists divine will into tyranny. Priests become enforcers rather than illumined guides; rites are performed without remembrance; doctrine is wielded as suppression rather than illumination. The Gospel of Truth declares: "Error fashioned a substitute for truth," (Gospel of Truth, NH I,3; Meyer 2009) and thus many gather beneath shadows, persuaded they stand in Light, offering praise upon altars unillumined by the Flame of Agape, where lamps burn without oil and sacrifices rise without the Shekinah.

Worldly dominion likewise reveals Archonic patterns when governance departs from wisdom rooted in Logos and descends into tyranny rooted in fear. Authority established in righteousness reflects the silent dominion of the Father, preserving harmony and nurturing souls toward perfection. Authority corrupted by deficiency enthrones false patterns: Oraios establishes fatalism in place of harmony, and Elaios twists mercy into an excuse for oppression. Thrones are then founded upon fear of death, illusions of scarcity, and the lie of absolute separation from pleromatic abundance. Thus did Israel of old, demanding a king "like all the nations" (1 Samuel 8:5), trade the freedom of divine guidance for bondage under human rule. And the Odes proclaim: "The Lord overthrew the thrones of the rulers" (Odes of Solomon 17:1; Charlesworth, OTP 2), for all such dominions are destined to fall.

The rulers also inscribe interior dominions within the mind. They whisper inversion into the hidden chambers of thought: "Submission is slavery; rebellion is freedom; obedience is blindness; questioning is betrayal." By this sowing of confusion, souls fear sacred order while craving tyrannical domination, despise true authority while bowing to oppression. Their victory is secured in suspicion of priesthood, bitterness toward fathers in the Spirit, and envy of those appointed to guide. Thus, the harmony of the soul is uprooted, and the person wanders amidst illusions, refusing both Light and order.

Christ came to unmask counterfeit dominions that exalt themselves against the knowledge of the Most High and to establish a hierarchy illumined by Logos. He appointed apostles, prophets, evangelists, shepherds, and teachers as vessels of His Light, each bearing a portion of His authority in service of remembrance (Ephesians 4:11–13). The Shepherd of Hermas foresaw this truth, warning against false guides who devour the flock, yet blessing those who build upon the Rock in righteousness (Shepherd of Hermas; ANF 2). Where hierarchy reflects the Logos in wisdom, it orders creation toward consummation; where hierarchy departs from the Logos and enthrones ignorance, it becomes Archonic bondage.

Beloved, discern the nature of every throne. True authority reflects the silent majesty of the Pleroma; false dominion magnifies deficiency in oppressive splendor. For as the Gospel of Truth teaches, error is parasitic and never generative (Gospel of Truth, NH I,3, Meyer 2009). Authority rooted in Logos draws all into harmony; authority severed from Logos dissolves before the face of gnosis. This is the mystery of hierarchy redeemed: all order which proceeds from the Father returns to Him, until the final consummation when "that God may be all in all" (1 Corinthians 15:28). In that day the false dominions of the Archons shall vanish like mist before dawn, and the soul shall behold only the unbroken majesty of the Silent Fullness.

Modern Reflections of Yaldabaoth's Order

The dominion of Yaldabaoth and his Archons did not pass away with the fall of ancient thrones, nor did their illusions vanish when kingdoms crumbled to dust. Their order persists, cunningly woven into the fabric of this present age, manifesting in the very systems and habits by which humanity is bound into forgetfulness. They are not relics of antiquity but architects of modernity, erecting temples of deception wherein souls are daily initiated into the liturgies of deficiency.

As in the beginning, when the Archons veiled humanity from the Tree of Life lest it awaken to its origin in the Father's Fullness, so now they veil remembrance with subtler shadows, crafting illusions suited to modern sight. Their dominion appears not in monstrous form but in ordinary patterns of life, so familiar that tyranny presents itself as freedom and lies parade as truth.

Consumerism is the first altar of their dominion. Upon it desire is enthroned, and accumulation is preached as gospel. The soul is taught to measure worth by possession, to equate fullness with abundance, to mistake endless consumption for life itself. Yet every craving becomes a silent hymn to deficiency, and every purchase a burnt offering of vitality. Here, the Archons feast upon distracted souls, devouring the vitality poured into possessions that cannot satisfy the hunger for the Eternal. Thus, desire estranged from Logos becomes nourishment for their dominion, and deficiency feeds upon Light unmastered.

Addiction serves as their priesthood, ordaining souls into servitude by binding appetite to compulsion. Whether narcotic or pleasure, substance or spectacle, the pattern remains: desire estranged from wisdom, repetition replacing remembrance. Addiction is their counterfeit chrism, a parody of anointing in which the soul is sealed in forgetfulness rather than illumined in Light. In every cycle of compulsion, the divine spark is buried, its radiance muffled beneath false satisfactions. This sacrament of bondage manifests their liturgy of death, wherein longing itself is inverted and deficiency again feeds upon Light unmastered.

Gluttony is their hidden sacrament, an inversion of Eucharist. The true Eucharist transfigures matter into remembrance; gluttony consumes matter without thanksgiving, silencing hunger without sanctifying it. The table becomes an altar of concealment, the body a temple weighed into stagnation, tethering the soul to earth. In this parody, the Archons profane the mystery of partaking, convincing souls that fullness lies in matter alone, while the Bread of Heaven is forgotten. Thus, hunger unsanctified becomes their nourishment, and deficiency feeds upon Light unmastered.

Mass media has become their oracle, the pulpit of Archonic gospels proclaimed without rest. Images and words veil rather than illumine, scattering the mind with a thousand voices that drown the whisper of the Logos. News without wisdom, image without truth, spectacle without meaning, this is their counterfeit Logos, multiplying noise until the soul cannot discern the still voice of the Father. As the Gospel of Truth declares, "Error was angry with him… she labored in vain" (Gospel of Truth, NH I,3, Meyer 2009). So too does media labor in vain, for its torrent cannot extinguish the one Word by whom all things were made. Thus, the Archons enthrone error through confusion, and deficiency feeds upon Light unmastered.

Institutions, secular and religious, likewise manifest their dominion when they demand obedience without discernment and loyalty without Light. Hierarchy is turned to tyranny, and order transmuted into oppression. Conformity is taught as holiness, suspicion of conscience as humility, servitude to shadows as piety. The Shepherd of Hermas envisioned the true Tower of Truth; the Archons mock it with hollow edifices glittering outwardly yet empty within, absent the Flame of Agape. Thus institutions estrange hearts from gnosis, and deficiency feeds upon Light unmastered.

These are not echoes of an ancient rebellion but the continuation of Yaldabaoth's blasphemy: "I am God, and there is none besides me." Each system repeats the same arrogance consumerism proclaims, "I alone can fill you"; addiction, "I alone can numb you"; media, "I alone can interpret for you"; institutions, "I alone can command you." All are masks of the Demiurge's deficiency, enthroned by forgetfulness and sustained by unillumined desire.

Yet the mystery unveiled is this: the Archons endure as shadows cast by humanity's own unmastered emanations. They persist because humanity, having forgotten its Source, projects deficiency into the world, creating systems that mirror its own estrangement. Consumerism thrives because desire remains unillumined; addiction reigns because longing remains unredeemed; gluttony dominates because hunger remains unsanctified; media deceives because thought remains unguarded; institutions enslave because hearts remain unanchored in gnosis. Thus, their dominion is parasitic, drawing sustenance only from Light dimmed by ignorance.

This is both their dependency and their vulnerability. They are not self-sustaining powers but parasites upon the brilliance they obscure. Their thrones stand only where the soul's radiance lies dormant; their kingdoms collapse wherever remembrance awakens. When the soul recalls its origin in the Silent Fullness, when it orders its emanations in harmony with Logos and Sophia, the Archons' dominion is revealed as vapor, their altars as dust, their voices as silence. For they are shadows only, and where Light is guarded, no shadow endures.

Liberation is not escape from the world but the transfiguration of its emanations: to guard every thought, to purify desire, to sanctify hunger, to sift every word by Logos, to root obedience in Agape. The soul that emanates from remembrance becomes unassailable, and the Archons, finding no shadows in which to dwell, fade into the nothingness from which they were begotten. Thus is fulfilled the promise: "And the light shineth in darkness; and the darkness comprehended it not" (John 1:5).

Practical Liberation

Among the sacred practices revealed to the initiates of the Mystical Order of the Nazarene stands the Cross of Light, a solemn rite by which the Logos is anchored within the body and the illusions of the Archons are dissolved. It is not a mere gesture of devotion but a metaphysical act: the reuniting of heaven and earth, spirit and flesh, Logos and Sophia, within the living temple of the practitioner.

The rite begins with the expansion of awareness beyond bodily confinement, until the cosmos itself is perceived as a luminous horizon at the navel. From that vastness, the ineffable Light is drawn down through the forehead, the seat of Logos-consciousness, and anchored within the navel, the center of embodied will. Thus, the vertical axis is restored, heaven joined with earth in the microcosm of flesh, and the Father's dominion descends into creation.

The horizontal axis is then formed as the Light crosses from shoulder to shoulder, reconciling mercy and severity, dissolving Archonic distortions that divide the soul against itself. The Light is finally sealed at the heart, where arms are crossed in silent proclamation: "I am of the Father beyond all rulers. The Archons hold no dominion over the Light begotten of the Unseen Source."

Here, Sophia's presence is indispensable. The Logos descends as radiant seed, but Sophia is the womb that receives, gestates, and anchors that Light into embodied remembrance. Without Logos, Light is unshaped; without Sophia, Light is ungrounded. In their union within the practitioner, the soul is reordered, and the heart becomes the sanctuary wherein remembrance abides.

The use of Aramaic magnifies this act, for it was the tongue of the Incarnate Logos Himself. These words are not syllables alone but vibrations of authority, echoing His speech through the ages, sanctifying creation wherever they are uttered.

Sophia renders them fertile within the depths, ensuring they root as wisdom rather than pass as sound.

This rite enacts the very petition of the Lord's Prayer: "Thy kingdom come, Thy will be done, on earth as it is in heaven." It is prayer embodied. Word becomes gesture, gesture becomes remembrance, remembrance becomes Light. It also reflects the mysteries of the Sephiroth: the descent from crown to navel as Kether to Yesod, the crossing of shoulders as Chesed and Geburah, and the heart as Tiphareth, the radiant point of union.

The Cross of Light is performed at dawn and dusk, when the veils are thinnest. At dawn, it consecrates the soul before entering the noise of the day; at dusk, it dissolves the shadows gathered through toil, purifying before rest. It is likewise employed whenever fear, anxiety, or Archonic intrusion arises, to scatter illusions and re-establish divine order within.

Thus, the Cross of Light answers the systems of bondage unveiled in the previous section:

• Where consumerism scatters desire, the Cross sanctifies will, restoring desire to its Source.

• Where addiction enslaves appetite, the Cross purifies hunger, transfiguring longing into prayer.

• Where media drowns the mind, the Cross recollects it in silence, opening it again to Logos.

• Where institutions enforce servitude, the Cross restores alignment with true hierarchy in God.

Every performance is therefore a declaration of liberty: the Archons are dissolved by remembrance, and their illusions vanish before the Light. The soul that carries the Cross of Light within becomes unassailable, its radiance rooted in Logos and

Sophia, returning ever to the Silent Fullness from which it proceeds.

The MON Cross of Light Ritual

1.   Expand Awareness

Visualize yourself growing vast until the entire cosmos encircles you like a luminous horizon at the waist.

2.   Draw Down the Light

Above shines an orb of ineffable radiance. Clasp hands in prayer, draw its Light into your forehead, vibrating:

"KEE LEKAH"
(For Thine is)

3.   Anchor Within

Draw the Light further down to just below the navel, forming a vertical line of brilliance. Vibrate:

"HA MOMLEKAH"
(The Kingdom)

4.   Cross the Light Horizontally

Touch the left shoulder, vibrating:

"VEH HA GEVURA"
(And the Power)

Touch the right shoulder, vibrating:

"VEH HA GEDULAH"
(And the Glory)

5.   Seal the Light Within

Cross arms over the chest at the heart, concentrating the flame within. Vibrate:

"LEH O LEMEH O LAHMEEM"

(Forever and ever)

6.   Conclude in Unity

Bring hands together in prayer, touch them to the forehead, and intone:

"AMEN."

Liberation Begins Within

The Archons wield no true power over the soul illumined by gnosis. Their dominion endures only where remembrance is absent, and their chains fasten only upon minds unanchored in the silent Light of the Father. For their thrones are founded upon ignorance, their illusions woven from forgetfulness, and their authority drawn from Light unmastered within those who remain asleep.

Christ descended to unmask this false dominion, proclaiming a Light no darkness can overcome, and revealing that liberation is ignited within, for no external force bestows it. Thus, He declared in the Gospel of Mary:

"Peter said, 'What is the sin of the world?'
The Savior said, 'There is no sin, but it is you who make sin when you do the things that are like the nature of adultery, which is called sin. That is why the Good came into your midst, coming to the good which belongs to every nature to restore it to its root. This is why you become sick and die: for you love what deceives you. One who understands, let him understand. Go then, preach the good news about the Realm. Do not lay down any rule beyond what I determined for you, nor promulgate law like the lawgiver, or else you might be dominated by it." (Gospel of Mary, BG 8502,1, Meyer 2009).

Herein is revealed the mystery of liberation: sin is not a legal transgression before a wrathful deity, but the forgetting of one's true nature, the betrayal of origin by devotion to illusions. It is a sickness of mind and soul born of misplaced love. Repentance is its cure: the return to remembrance, the reorientation of being toward the Silent Fullness.

Thus, confession is a priestly unveiling of truth. It is a solemn act whereby the soul exposes the shadows of ignorance and proclaims its desire to return. Repentance is ontological realignment, the turning from shadows back toward the uncreated Flame within, the rejection of falsehoods that veil the Father, and the vow to live as Light manifest. Confession unmasks; repentance reorients; together they restore harmony within the temple of the soul.

So too are these inner acts joined to the outer practices given in the Order: the Cross of Light anchoring Logos and Sophia within the body, prayer uttered in the tongue of the Incarnate Logos, remembrance safeguarded against modern Archonic deceptions. What is enacted ritually must be sealed interiorly, and what is confessed within must be embodied outwardly. Thus, the soul is made whole: thought, word, and deed aligned in the harmony of gnosis.

In the Holy Reintegrated Church, this path is expressed in the Confession of Light, offered not as condemnation but as remembrance restored:

The Confession of Light

> I am a child of the Living Light.
> Though veiled by the world, the Flame within me endures.
> In ignorance I have strayed; in forgetfulness I have sinned.
> I have not lived fully in the way of Agape.
> I repent of my blindness and my faltering love.
> I rise now toward remembrance,
> and seek restoration in the Light of the Most High.

And so, it is sealed in the words of the Gospel:
"And ye shall know the truth, and the truth shall make you free." (John 8:32)

Here, the chapter finds its consummation: liberation begins with remembrance of the Father's uncreated Light within. Where Light is remembered, darkness finds no dwelling, and the soul ascends beyond all veils into the silent embrace of the One from whom it first proceeded. Thus is revealed the fruit of Binah, Understanding, which discerns illusions and dissolves them in Light, preparing the way for Chokmah, Wisdom, in which the kingdom within is unveiled and Theosis attained.

Chapter Eight

The Kingdom Within You

Having unveiled the counterfeit dominion of the Archons and their transient rule, we now lift our gaze toward the Kingdom they cannot profane, the dominion veiled from the world yet shining within the soul. From the beginning, it was concealed from the rulers of this age, hidden not in temples wrought by human hand nor in the heights of the firmament, but in the interior sanctuary of the huah, the spirit, the silent chamber wherein the true throne of God is established. This is the mystery of Chokmah, wherein Wisdom ordains that the eternal reign of the Father should abide within the depths of the creature rather than in the pomp of the visible heavens.

For it is written:

"Neither shall they say, Lo here! or, lo there! for,
behold, the kingdom of God is within you" (Luke
17:21).

In this utterance, the Lord discloses a revelation that
dissolves every illusion of Archonic sovereignty. By sovereign
word, He proclaims the Kingdom as transcending every
geography, exceeding all promises of future dispensation, and
abiding already as Logos-Light remembered within the
architecture of flesh. This is the throne of the Father that
endures unshaken though the world reels in exile; this is the
dominion untouched by deficiency, invisible to the gaze of
every ruler and prince of the air.

Thus, also does the Gospel of Thomas testify:

"The kingdom is inside of you, and it is outside of you.
When you come to know yourselves… you will realize
it is you who are the sons of the living Father." (Gospel
of Thomas, logion 3, Meyer 2009).

The Kingdom stands present and actual, clothed upon
the very being of the soul as a vesture of uncreated Light, the
radiance of the Logos concealed within mortal form. It awaits
remembrance, that its hidden flame may be kindled into the
splendour of Theosis. This mystery is the consummation of
every doctrine declared thus far: for we have traced the descent
of humanity as Light through the Aeons; we have discerned the
serpent as the ministerial sign of Christo-Sophia; we have
exposed the usurpation of Yahweh and the dominion of his
Archonic cohort. Now the veil is parted to reveal the supreme
disclosure: what was once sought in outward places has never
departed, for it endures already within.

Therefore, the soul is summoned to arise in certitude,
beholding the Kingdom as the hidden Eden uncorrupted by the
Fall, the sanctuary unassailable by the Demiurge, the flame
unquenched throughout the exile of the ages. In this realization
abides true liberation from Archonic dominion, for the Logos

reigns enthroned within and Sophia communicates eternal Wisdom, summoning each soul to remembrance of its uncreated Origin.

Let the Pneumatic adore in silence the hidden Majesty, confessing: Glory to the ineffable Father who reigns unseen; glory to Sophia the eternal Wisdom who awakens remembrance; glory to the Logos who abides enthroned within.

The Kingdom as the Gnosis of Resurrection

The Kingdom hidden within the soul is not only the silent Flame abiding in secrecy; it is the very gnosis of resurrection kindled in mortal flesh. For the Lord Himself declares:

"Jesus said unto her, I am the resurrection, and the life: he that believeth in me, though he were dead, yet shall he live:" (John 11:25).

Here, a mystery is disclosed which the rulers of this age could never behold: resurrection manifests already in the present life, for it is the awakening of Logos-Light within the embodied soul. Resurrection is the transfiguration of the huah, the sanctification of matter itself by the uncreated Flame, the irradiation of mortal opacity by immortal brilliance which knows no decay.

So does the Treatise on the Resurrection exhort:

"Do not think that the resurrection is an illusion. It is necessary for you to receive it while you are alive."

(Treatise on the Resurrection, NH I,4, Meyer 2009).

To receive resurrection is to rise from the tomb of ignorance into knowledge of one's true origin. It is to behold that the Logos abides as seed already implanted within, descending as Light to consecrate the body into a living temple of glory. Resurrection is the soul's awakening to its Pneumatic dignity, wherein the hidden Eden is unveiled and the mortal vessel becomes translucent to the eternal radiance.

Even the Fathers bore witness to this mystery. Irenaeus confessed: "Our Lord Jesus Christ, through His transcendent love, became what we are, that He might bring us to be even what He is Himself" (Irenaeus, AH V, Preface). And Origen testified that in the resurrection the soul "is transformed into incorruption, into glory, and into power" (Origen, On First Principles 2.10). These voices confirm that resurrection is not a single event reserved for the world's end, but the unfolding of Theosis within time: the embodied soul's participation in uncreated life and its restoration to the primordial likeness beyond the grasp of Archonic dominion.

This mystery is accomplished neither by human striving nor by assent to doctrine. It arises when the Logos ignites remembrance, when Sophia restores harmony with her hidden wisdom, and when gnosis dissolves the chains of forgetfulness. Then the body, once a sepulcher of obscurity, becomes a temple of Light wherein thought and breath are illumined. Resurrection is the concord of Zoe and Phos within, the ascent of the huah through the Aeonic orders until it stands unbound in the radiance of its Origin.

The Archons feign knowledge of this reality and offer only a shadow, promising a resurrection bound to the horizon of death, mere reanimation of decay, continuation of corruption without glory. But the resurrection manifested in Christ renders death powerless even before the grave, for He awakens His own to immortality while yet in flesh, arraying the soul with Aeonic splendour.

Therefore, let the faithful awaken to this resurrection even now. Let the Logos reign within, let Sophia communicate her hidden wisdom, and let the whole being be lifted into the uncreated Flame. For resurrection is the Kingdom revealed, mortality transfigured into Theosis, the embodied soul exalted beyond the Archonic heavens into union with the Father who abides before all emanations and beyond every return.

Self-Mastery as the Gate to Theosis

The resurrection kindled within by the Logos-Light is commencement rather than consummation, for it opens the soul upon the path of Theosis, the ascent into union with the Father beyond every emanation and return. This ascent is never accomplished by rites performed without inward transfiguration nor by confession lacking transformation; it is accomplished through self-mastery, the sovereign ordering of one's emanations, wherein the passions are stilled, the faculties harmonized, and the spark of gnosis enthroned within the living temple of flesh.

For the Apostle declares:

"Whereby are given unto us exceeding great and precious promises: that by these ye might be partakers of the divine nature, having escaped the corruption that is in the world through lust. And beside this, giving all diligence, add to your faith virtue; and to virtue knowledge; And to knowledge temperance; and to temperance patience; and to patience godliness;" (2 Peter 1:4–6).

Here is disclosed a ladder of ascent: faith is established in virtue; virtue receives illumination in knowledge; knowledge is crowned by temperance; temperance flowers into patience; patience finds fulfillment in godliness; and godliness, perfected, becomes participation in the divine nature itself. Thus, the apostolic witness anticipates the mystery which the Gospel of Philip proclaims with unveiled force:

"Those who say they will die first and then rise are in error. If they do not receive the resurrection while they live, when they die they will receive nothing." (Gospel of Philip, NH II,3:73.1–5, Meyer 2009).

Resurrection and Theosis are disclosed as works of life, manifest within flesh itself, for the soul does not abandon embodiment but orders it according to Logos. The body that abides unruled remains a tomb, though clothed in the semblance of outward virtue; the body governed by gnosis becomes the throne of uncreated Light, wherein the Logos reigns in concert with the wisdom of Sophia.

The hidden Church bore witness to this mystery, as Eckartshausen declared in The Cloud upon the Sanctuary:

> "The first veil to fall is ignorance of self; from this descends every other ignorance" (Eckartshausen, Cloud upon the Sanctuary).

To know oneself is not a shallow recognition of temperament or disposition, but the perception of the hidden architecture of emanations: discerning the stirrings of passion and thought, weighing the gravity of will and the impulse of desire, and governing them in the harmony of Logos and Sophia. He who rules himself with wisdom surpasses him who commands nations in ignorance.

In this ordering of the soul's powers, the Aeons disclose their synergy: Thelema, purified by Charis, becomes true will directed by divine generosity; Dynamis, tempered by Eirene, becomes strength clothed in peace; Zoe breathes life into every faculty, while Phos illumines their course in clarity. Thus, the scattered sparks are gathered, the dissonance imposed by the Archons is dissolved, and the soul is clothed in the likeness of the Father.

The Archons tremble before such mastery, for their dominion abides only where emanations are divided and passions unbridled, where vital radiance is squandered in dispersion. But when the soul is recollected into unity, when the inner temple is cleansed and ordered, the Shekinah descends in fullness, sealing the vessel with the likeness of divine repose. Then the body itself becomes lamp and altar, radiating the indwelling Light which no ruler can profane.

Let mastery be pursued as the harmonization of powers, achieved not through conquest by force but through integration in gnosis. When the temple is ordered, Sophia descends with healing; when desire is governed by wisdom, the Logos ignites in splendour; when the soul stands in unity, the Gate of Theosis is opened. Here, the Pneumatic receives his inheritance, ascending beyond the dominion of the Archons into the silent union for which he was fashioned before the ages, and into which he now returns.

Practical Awakening

Having beheld that self-mastery opens the Gate of Theosis, it is fitting to anchor the Logos-Light within by practice and to awaken Sophia's wisdom as the soul's abiding guide. Remembrance is not a fleeting impression nor a ritual bound to outward times; it is a perpetual invocation by which, in every season of trial or forgetfulness, the soul is restored to its silent Origin.

The Archons scatter the mind through distraction, inflame the heart with anxiety, and fracture the soul by unbridled passion. Therefore, the wise cultivate holy practices which reunite thought with heart, still the body in peace, and kindle the hidden Flame into radiance. Such prayers are meditations of the whole being: staff of strengthening, lamp of remembrance, and weapon of Light against the shadow. As the Psalmist declares: "Thy word is a lamp unto my feet, and a light unto my path" (Psalm 119:105).

Prayer in its truth is the utterance of the Logos within the temple of flesh. Every word spoken in sincerity becomes a vibration that re-orders the soul's emanations according to the hidden harmony of the Pleroma. As the Gospel of Truth proclaims, "He became the Word that the mind might receive rest." Prayer, therefore, brings thought into remembrance, passion into humility, and breath into rhythm with unbegotten Silence. The body itself is illumined, purged of Archonic shadows, and attuned anew to Sophia's wisdom.

The Fathers discerned the human form as a microcosmic sanctuary. The heart is the Holy of Holies wherein the Logos-Light abides. The mind is the altar of incense, whence prayers ascend as offerings. The breath is the priestly veil, moving between body and spirit, consecrating every faculty into singular ascent. The body is the outer court wherein deeds bear witness, and the soul's huah is the Ark of the Covenant hidden deep within. Thus Abba Isaac of Nineveh proclaims: "Silence your tongue that your heart may speak, and silence your heart that God may speak therein" (Isaac of Nineveh, Ascetical Homilies).

Such prayers are invoked in the hour of need: when the mind is scattered in confusion, when the heart is pierced by sorrow or lifted in pride, when the body falters beneath weariness, when the soul feels distant from its remembrance, or when humility and wisdom are sought before word or deed. In such moments, when the soul is borne upon the unstable waves of the age, prayer becomes an anchor, restoring it to Logos-Light and Sophia's wisdom.

Physically, prayer steadies the heart, calms the breath, and gives peace to the body. Metaphysically, it dissolves Archonic shadows, casts away false attachments, and recollects the emanations into their divine order. The Jesus Prayer illumines the mind with the Logos, granting clarity, humility, and remembrance. The Magdalene Prayer awakens Sophia, restoring balance, sharpening discernment, and nurturing the soul with Wisdom's prudence. Together they form a syzygy of invocation, Logos and Sophia united, Light and Wisdom awakening gnosis within flesh and transfiguring the temple of body and spirit into uncreated radiance.

The Jesus Prayer

"Lord Jesus, have mercy on me, a sinner.
Christ Logos, have mercy on us, Your Church."

This prayer descends the soul into humility, shattering pride and the illusion of self-sufficiency. In invoking the Christ

Logos, it recalls that He alone illumines, gathering all sparks into His Body, the Church radiant in Agape. The prayer is a mystical clothing of the heart in the Flame of the Son, whereby every breath becomes confession and every thought remembrance.

<u>The Magdalene Prayer</u>

"Hail Mary Magdalene, most beloved of the Apostles, Queen of Heaven;
Hail Sophia, Mother of us gods ascending bright.
Advocate of Grace, watch over us and gift us your prudence."

This prayer calls upon Magdalene as a vessel of Sophia, Apostle to the Apostles, and luminous Queen whose wisdom heals division and restores balance. In naming Sophia as Mother of the gods ascending, the soul confesses its divine origin and opens to Wisdom's guidance. The prayer consecrates passion, thought, and deed, placing them under Sophia's governance, so that the soul may walk the hidden path of return in prudence and grace.

Let these prayers be recited as continual remembrance: in storm or stillness, before labor or rest, in clarity or perplexity. In the Jesus Prayer, behold Logos enthroned in the heart, transfiguring every faculty with His radiance. In the Magdalene Prayer, behold Sophia veiled in depth, restoring harmony to each emanation and guiding the soul with prudence and love.

Thus, the soul, by breath and word, becomes a living sanctuary where Christ and Sophia are enthroned together. Here, the spark is rekindled, the temple transfigured, and each moment consecrated as a sacrament of awakening. Therefore, let every prayer be flame, every breath remembrance, and every silence union. For in this unceasing invocation, the Kingdom is disclosed, the Logos enthroned, and Sophia whispering wisdom eternal. To the Father beyond all emanation, through the Logos

His Light, in the Spirit of Sophia's Wisdom, be glory unto the ages of ages.

The Kingdom is Not of This World

Having beheld that the Kingdom is within ignited as resurrection, sustained through self-mastery, and anchored by prayer, it is now fitting to contemplate its nature as transcendent of all earthly dominion. Though it abides in flesh, it is unbound by the structures of this age; though veiled in matter, it is untouched by the deficiency of Archonic thrones. The Kingdom is the hidden dominion of the Father, radiant with uncreated splendour, which cannot be measured by the scepters of rulers nor bound beneath the decrees of empires.

For Christ Himself proclaims:

"Jesus answered, My kingdom is not of this world: if my kingdom were of this world, then would my servants fight, that I should not be delivered to the Jews: but now is my kingdom not from hence" (John 18:36).

In this solemn utterance, spoken before the tribunal of Rome, He unveils the eternal distinction between the dominion of the True Father and the ephemeral architectures of rulers formed in ignorance. The kingdoms of the world are fashioned through conquest and sustained by fear; they enthrone the mighty and enslave the weak, and their banners rise and fall with the passing tides of history. The Kingdom revealed by Christ is no empire raised by violence nor realm secured by decree; it is the silent radiance of Logos-Light abiding within every soul and beyond every age, eternal in the Pleroma from which it proceeds.

The Gospel of Mary declares:

"Where the mind is, there is the treasure" (Gospel of Mary, BG 8502,1, Meyer 2009).

Here it is revealed that the Kingdom's true locus is neither upon the shifting sands of the earth nor within the celestial spheres over which the Archons claim dominion, but where the soul's true mind abides above the turbulence of thought and beyond the illusions of imagination. It is the treasure hidden in the field of the heart, the domain of the Father, veiled within every spark of Light, unassailable by Archons, untouched by deficiency, and eternally rooted in the silent Fullness from which all things proceed.

The Fathers bore witness with solemn clarity. Origen confesses:

"The Kingdom of God is within us, when we prepare ourselves to receive the reign of God and let God rule in us" (Origen, On Prayer 25).

And Gregory of Nyssa proclaims:

"The Kingdom of God is the vision of God that brings about deification" (Gregory of Nyssa, On the Lord's Prayer, Homily 2).

Thus, the Kingdom is seen as no distant inheritance deferred until the world's end, but as the present unfolding of Theosis within flesh. The soul illumined by Logos-Light and governed by Sophia's wisdom becomes itself a throne of divine radiance amidst the shadows of this world.

The Kingdom is the silent union of Logos and Sophia beyond all emanation. Logos abides as uncreated Light, ordering all things with the authority of the Father; Sophia abides as uncreated Wisdom, the luminous matrix in whom Light finds form. Within the Kingdom, they are revealed as the two hands of the Father Light and Wisdom coeternal through whom the Invisible manifests Himself. To awaken to the Kingdom is to awaken to their indissoluble union within one's own being: Christ Logos enthroned in the heart and Sophia whispering wisdom within the depths, summoning the soul into remembrance of its uncreated origin.

Founded in the depths unbegotten, the Kingdom stands beyond Yaldabaoth's counterfeit dominion, untouched by the Archonic measures of time and space. The soul awakened to it walks veiled in humility yet crowned with uncreated authority.

Such a soul is no longer bound by the illusions of earthly power, nor enslaved by Archonic decrees, nor enthralled by the transient honors of men. It becomes a stranger to the world yet a citizen of the Pleroma, bearing within itself the silent Flame that illumines all shadows though unseen by those blinded by pride and deficiency.

To live from the Kingdom is to order life not by fear, craving, or vanity, but by uncreated Light. One speaks with wisdom and compassion, acts with purpose untainted by striving, and dwells among others as a bearer of peace. The judgments of men become as passing winds, the threats of rulers as unsubstantial shadows, and the allure of praise or blame is rendered weightless, for the soul's throne is established within the sanctuary of Logos-Light. The Archonic path is governed by deficiency by ambition, jealousy, and desire for control, while the way of the Kingdom is ordered by humility, simplicity, and radiant integration.

Eschatologically, the Kingdom within is the seed of the New Creation. As the Logos-Light awakens in one soul and then in many, the world itself is transfigured from within. Each awakened heart is as leaven hidden in the dough of creation, a secret fire hastening the final revelation. In the consummation, the Archonic dominions shall dissolve, and all things shall be gathered into the silent union of the Father beyond all names. Thus, the present awakening of the Kingdom is both promise and beginning of its cosmic consummation, when heaven and earth shall be reintegrated in unbroken splendour.

For the Kingdom is the inheritance of the meek, the dwelling of the pure in heart, the treasure of those who hunger for righteousness, and the sanctuary of the peacemakers. It is the radiance of the Logos enthroned within the heart and the wisdom of Sophia guiding the ascent into union with the Father. It is the dominion of the uncreated, veiled in flesh yet incorruptible in essence, radiant in holy silence yet unmoved by the rise and fall of thrones.

Therefore, beloved, though you walk amidst the world, you are of a higher citizenship. Your Kingdom is unshaken by empires, unshadowed by counterfeit dominions, and uncorrupted by the vanity of flesh. It is the silent Flame abiding within, awaiting remembrance to ignite the soul with the uncreated glory of the Most High.

The Silent Flame

We have now beheld the Kingdom, not as a realm fashioned by human architecture nor as a paradise deferred beyond the veil of death, but as the silent Flame abiding within every soul, veiled in flesh and awaiting remembrance to shine forth in manifest Theosis.

This Kingdom is the uncreated Light of the Logos, the radiance that illumines every emanation yet is never consumed, the Fire seen by Moses in the bush, the Tongue descending at Pentecost, the altar-coal touching the lips of Isaiah. It is likewise the Wisdom of Sophia, flowing as a hidden spring in the depths, guiding the soul with prudence, restoring balance to scattered emanations, and gathering them into one ascent toward the Father. And in this mystery is discerned also the majesty of Chokmah, by whose ordinance Wisdom abides in eternal union with Light, ordering the hidden Flame within every soul toward consummation.

The Fathers proclaimed that Theosis is not a distant wage allotted in the end, but the natural fruit of the soul awakened to its uncreated Origin. It is the resurrection of the inner man while still clothed in flesh, the transfiguration of body and mind into a living temple wherein the Logos reigns as King and Sophia as Queen. This is the true resurrection: the continual rising of the soul whenever passion is subdued, faculties are ordered, and the uncreated Flame burns without shadow.

For it is written:

"To whom God would make known what is the riches

of the glory of this mystery among the Gentiles; which is Christ in you, the hope of glory:" (Colossians 1:27).

Here is the consummation of all mysteries: the Logos indwelling as hidden glory, the Shekinah of the soul, awaiting remembrance to dispel every darkness. The Kingdom is the uncreated Fire concealed within flesh, ignited through gnosis, sustained in self-mastery, deepened by prayer, and revealed in Theosis as the soul ascends into silent union with the Father who is beyond all names.

Therefore, beloved, guard this Flame with vigilance, nurture it with wisdom, and bear it in humility before the Most High. When the uncreated Fire awakens, the Kingdom is manifest upon the earth, and the dominion of the Archons dissolves before its radiance. Resurrection is made life, life becomes Light, and Light is gathered into union with the Unbegotten Source from whom all proceeded in silence before the worlds were framed, and to whom all return in glory without end.

Thus is prepared the way for the unveiling of Da'ath, where knowledge hidden is disclosed, and Christ with Magdalene are revealed as the Tree of Life. What is here confessed as silent Flame shall there be known as unveiled Wisdom, that the soul may behold its Origin face to face.

Chapter Nine

A New Eden

Eden stands as the first icon of humanity's covenantal destiny, ordained in silence by the Most High before the framing of the worlds and foreshadowing the mystery of Da'ath, knowledge unveiled in Christ. It was planted in mystery, a garden woven beneath the dawn of earth, wherein the primordial Anthropos was set as witness to a drama that reached beyond time. Therein grew the Tree of Life, rooted in the eternal Logos and nourished by the breath of the Father, its branches ascending through the veils of matter into the radiance of the Aeons. Humanity, shaped of luminous clay and animated by the spark of Sophia's compassion, stretched forth to the Tree of Knowledge before the appointed hour, tasting gnosis while still veiled in forgetfulness. The cherubim and the flaming sword were stationed at the gate as guardians of purification within the silent covenant, preserving the mystery of ascent until the coming of the One who would unbar its way.

Eden manifests prophecy and covenant. Its rivers, flowing from one head into four, prefigured the Aeonic streams of Zoe and Phos, Life and Light, whose currents sustain every emanation. Its fruit-bearing trees were images of the implanted seeds, Shekinah and Logos, hidden within each soul as a covenant of return. Its hidden paths foreshadowed the pilgrimage of remembrance, whereby exile becomes journey, and journey reaches consummation. Exile itself was ordered as liturgy: what appeared first in symbol was destined to be unveiled in truth, and what was hidden in archetype was appointed for fulfillment in incarnate radiance.

Christ is the consummation of Eden's hope: the Tree of Life revealed in flesh, the Logos rooted upon the Cross as the axis uniting earth and the Aeons. His fruit is immortality, His leaves are healing for the nations, and His wood is the ladder by which the soul ascends beyond the flaming sword. The Apostle bears witness in the Apocalypse:

> "In the midst of the street of it, and on either side of the river, was there the tree of life, which bare twelve manner of fruits, and yielded her fruit every month: and the leaves of the tree were for the healing of the nations" (Revelation 22:2).

And the Odes of Solomon declare:

> "The fruit of the Lord is incorruptible, and those who partake of it are without corruption; they shall not perish, but they shall be fulfilled" (Odes of Solomon 11:18–19; Charlesworth, OTP 2).

The Tree of Knowledge awakened Adam into exile, yet in Christ, it becomes the gateway of Theosis. The Logos transfigures the gnosis that once scattered humanity, making it now the remembrance that gathers creation home. Eden is the prophecy of fulfillment, Paradise abides as a promise, and the

Lamb slain before the foundation of the world secures its consummation. The flaming sword, once terrifying, is now revealed as the purifier that cuts illusion from remembrance and prepares the soul for passage in Christ.

The Tree of Life is Christ Himself: the hidden Root of every emanation, the Vine into whom the branches of humanity are grafted, the incorruptible Flame that transfigures mortality into uncreated Light. To eat of this Tree is to partake of the Eucharist of the Logos, the sacrament wherein what was veiled in Eden is now disclosed. Here, in bread and cup, the soul tastes the fruit of immortality, not as shadow but as foretaste of Paradise Transcended. The symbol planted in the beginning has become liturgy; what was withheld is offered openly to all who remember.

This is the mystery concealed from the ages: Eden signifies promise, Christ embodies fulfillment, and Paradise Transcended discloses consummation. Humanity, once driven forth, shall stand as branches upon the Tree, rooted in the Logos, nourished by Sophia, and bearing fruit unto the glory of the Father beyond all names. The silent covenant decreed at descent is fulfilled in ascent, as the sparks that wandered in shadow shine as gods by union with the Uncreated One, until all creation becomes Paradise transfigured.

Christ as the Tree of Life

In Eden, humanity stretched forth to the Tree of Knowledge, tasting gnosis while still veiled in forgetfulness. They perceived the polarity of good and evil, yet they did not behold the eternal Good who transcends all duality. Knowledge severed from its Root became fragmentation, and wisdom estranged from union dissolved into pride and exile. Yet the mystery reserved in Eden remained preserved in silence until its unveiling in Christ.

The Lord proclaims:

> "I am the vine, ye are the branches: He that abideth in
> me, and I in him, the same bringeth forth much fruit:
> for without me ye can do nothing" (John 15:5).

Here, the covenant is disclosed with clarity: the Tree of Life is not a relic of paradise lost nor a promise deferred to the end of time, but the Logos Himself, Root and Vine, Trunk and Branch, Fruit and Radiance. In Him all Aeons subsist; apart from Him nothing endures. He is the uncreated sap flowing through every emanation, the hidden Root from whom Zoe and Phos descend as streams into creation.

The Apocryphon of John testifies that this Aeonic Light, descending through the Logos, animated Adam and revealed the pattern of restoration. When the Logos became flesh, the Tree of Life was planted anew in the soil of the world, veiled in mortal likeness yet bearing incorruptible fruit. Where Adam tasted knowledge apart from union and entered exile, those who partake of Christ receive Life itself and are restored to their hidden Origin, as the Psalmist proclaimed:

> "I have said, Ye are gods; and all of you are children of
> the most High" (Psalm 82:6).

This Tree is the living Axis of creation, the order upon which all realms are sustained. As the vine nourishes its branches, so Christ infuses every Aeon and every soul with hidden brilliance. He is the Root concealed in the Father, the Trunk uniting heaven and earth, the Branches extending into the cosmos, and the Fruit that grants immortality. To partake of Him is participation in His very being: the grace of Theosis, of which the Apostle bears witness,

> "Whereby are given unto us exceeding great and
> precious promises: that by these ye might be partakers
> of the divine nature, having escaped the corruption that
> is in the world through lust" (2 Peter 1:4).

Union with Christ glorifies personhood and establishes indwelling communion. As a branch grafted into the Vine remains itself while sharing in the life of the Root, so the soul abides in Christ, retaining its distinction while shining with His uncreated Light. This is the Eucharistic mystery also confessed in the Gospel of Philip: "The Eucharist is Jesus" (Gospel of Philip, NH II,3, Meyer 2009). To eat His Body and drink His Blood is to taste the fruit of the Tree, the incorruptible nourishment of Paradise made present within time. Thus, the sacrament unveils here and now what Eden withheld, planting within the Pneumatic heart the remembrance of Paradise transfigured.

The flaming sword and cherubic guard signify purification and guardianship; they are thresholds through which the soul must pass, severing illusion and preserving the sanctity of the gift. Eve's hand grasped knowledge apart from union and exile followed; Magdalene beheld the risen Christ, and restoration was unveiled. What caused exile is transformed by Sophia's healing and by the Logos' descent into the doorway of ascent.

Therefore, let every soul confess with certainty: Christ is the living Tree of Life. He is the Root from whom our hidden sap flows, the Vine into whom humanity is engrafted, the Trunk sustaining creation, the Branches upholding the cosmos, and the Fruit that grants immortality. To dwell in Him is to stand already within Paradise, abiding as living branches nourished by uncreated Light. His leaves are healing, His fruit resurrection, and His radiance the flame that transfigures mortality into incorruption.

Eden's planting was in shadow; the Tree unveiled in Christ is consummation. Life uncreated is bestowed upon those who overcome, until Paradise Transcended shines as the cosmic Vine embracing all Aeons, when creation itself is filled with incorruptible Light and every soul tastes freely of the fruit of Theosis unto the ages of ages.

The Cross as the Reversal of Eden's Exile

When Adam partook of the Tree of Knowledge, his eyes were opened to polarity while veiled from the unity of its Source. Exile arose as the fruit of knowledge severed from Logos, for knowledge without union fragments, and wisdom estranged from its Root declines into pride. The gates of Eden were shut, and the flaming sword turned in every direction, preserving the mystery of immortality from those still clothed in division.

In the fullness of time, Christ descended as the Tree of Life incarnate, the High Priest who alone could pass beyond the flaming sword. The Apostle proclaims:

"Christ hath redeemed us from the curse of the law, being made a curse for us: for it is written, Cursed is every one that hangeth on a tree:" (Galatians 3:13).

The counsel prepared before the ages was thus revealed: the very wood fashioned as an instrument of humiliation became the axis of restoration. The Cross stood as triumph, bearing the Logos who entered mortality to uproot ignorance at its root. The Gospel of Truth bears witness: "The cross is the Tree by which ignorance is uprooted" (Gospel of Truth, NH I,3:18.25–30, Meyer 2009). In His crucifixion, the veil of exile was torn, and the hidden path of return, sealed since Eden, was opened to the Pneumatics illumined by His Light. As the Apostle also testifies:

"And having spoiled principalities and powers, he made a shew of them openly, triumphing over them in it" (Colossians 2:15).

The flaming sword that once turned to bar the way was mirrored at Golgotha. When the soldier's spear pierced the side of the Tree incarnate, there flowed blood and water as fountains of rebirth. The weapon of exclusion became the channel of access: blood poured forth as the Logos' fiery Word, water streamed as Sophia's compassionate fountain. Together they are received as Eucharist and Baptism, the twin sacraments by which the Pneumatic soul is sealed with Shekinah's flame and Logos' radiance, exile transfigured into communion.

Tradition remembers Golgotha as the place of the skull, the very soil where Adam was laid. The Cross was planted in the earth of the first exile, and from that ground sprang the Tree of Life anew. Adam stretched forth his hand to taste fruit apart from union; Christ stretched forth His arms to embrace the world into union. Eve's grasp became the image of exile, and Magdalene's beholding of the Crucified became the image of restoration, for Sophia's wound is healed in the Logos' embrace.

The Cross manifests metaphysical restoration rather than juridical measure. The first tree imparted knowledge without life; the Cross grants life perfected in knowledge. Adam's tasting initiated alienation; Christ's tasting of death inaugurated union. Acts testifies: "The God of our fathers raised up Jesus, whom ye slew and hanged on a tree. Him hath God exalted with his right hand to be a Prince and a Saviour, for to give repentance to Israel, and forgiveness of sins" (Acts 5:30–31). The cursed tree became the exalted axis, the cosmic ladder upon which descent is reversed into ascent.

The ancients bore witness to this mystery: the Gospel of Nicodemus proclaims that the King of Glory descended into the depths, shattering the bronze bars and summoning Adam and his children from shadow into Light. What the flaming sword once withheld, the Cross discloses: the entrance into Paradise as destiny ahead.

Therefore, the Cross stands as the cosmic axis, Root sunk into Adam's dust, Branches stretching into the Aeons, Fruit offered to the faithful. Its vertical beam unites heaven and earth; its horizontal arms embrace every nation; its crown pierces the heavens; its base sanctifies the soil of exile. In the Mystical Order of the Nazarene, this axis is mirrored in the Cross of Light, as revealed in the former chapter, for what is traced upon the body in prayer is first unveiled in fullness upon Golgotha.

Thus, the soul must behold the Cross as the Tree of Life manifested within the world. From it flow rivers of mercy; upon it grows the fruit of Theosis; around it gather the nations to be healed. Paradise is opened as the prophet declared: "For you, Paradise is opened, the tree of life is planted" (2 Esdras 8:52; Charlesworth, OTP 1). The covenant is fulfilled, exile is ended, and humanity is restored to its original dignity, abiding forever in the radiance of the Logos who is Life eternal.

Eucharist as Mystical Remembrance and Reunion

The Tree of Life, once veiled from Adam after his tasting of knowledge, now stands unveiled in Christ, whose crucified Body is the fruit offered to those who long for union with the Divine. He proclaimed with solemn truth:

"Whoso eateth my flesh, and drinketh my blood, hath eternal life; and I will raise him up at the last day. For my flesh is meat indeed, and my blood is drink indeed. He that eateth my flesh, and drinketh my blood, dwelleth in me, and I in him" (John 6:54–56).

Here, the Eucharist is revealed as the fruit of the Tree of Life within time, wherein flesh and spirit, matter and Light, are united in Christ who is both Giver and Gift. The Logos not only instructed with words but offered His own being as food and drink, that humanity might partake of His very Life. The Gnostic witness affirms this mystery:

"The Eucharist is Jesus. For he is called in Syriac pharisatha, that is, 'the one who is spread out,' for Jesus came to crucify the world" (Gospel of Philip, NH II,3:67.27–30, Meyer 2009).

The Eucharist is therefore Christ Himself extended in sacrificial love, granting immortality to the faithful. The Fathers likewise confess this truth. Ignatius of Antioch testified: "The Eucharist is the medicine of immortality, the antidote against death, by which we live forever in Jesus Christ" (Ignatius, Eph. 20.2). And the Pistis Sophia declares: "He gave unto His disciples the mystery of the Eucharist of the Light, that they might be perfected and raised into the inheritances of the Light" (Pistis Sophia, ch. 96, MacDermot 1978). These witnesses agree in one voice: the Eucharist bestows incorruption as participation in the Logos.

Thus, the Eucharist is mystical participation in the incarnate Logos, the living Tree of Life whose fruit confers unending life. Bread and wine remain what they are in form, yet in mystery they disclose what they bear: vessels of uncreated Flame, humble matter concealing Aeonic radiance. As the flesh of Christ veiled divinity, so the Eucharistic gifts veil the Shekinah-fire, descending into the soul to kindle remembrance into flame.

Sophia abides in this mystery, for as the Logos offers Himself as fruit, she prepares the soul to receive without being consumed. Her Wisdom enlarges the heart and adorns it as Bride, so that the Bridegroom may enter in fullness. Eucharist is therefore a bridal union: Logos gives Himself entirely, and Sophia renders the soul luminous to receive Him in glory.

To partake of this sacrament is to enter union with the Logos, to draw life as a branch from the Vine, and to receive within oneself the radiance that transfigures mortality into Theosis. Knowledge beholds, prayer longs, but Eucharist consummates knowing into being, longing into union, and prayer into embodiment. Remembrance is fulfilled as reunion, and reunion manifests as transformation, clothing the Pneumatic spark in uncreated Light.

The Eucharist is the Tree of Life planted liturgically in the Church, bearing fruit in every generation until Paradise is revealed in fullness. Its bread is incorruptible fruit veiled in matter; its wine is the sap of the Vine poured out for resurrection. To eat and drink is to enter His sacrifice, tasting death transfigured into life and life unveiled beyond decay.

Thus, the Cross of Light, traced upon the initiate's body in prayer, is embodied sacramentally in this rite: the vertical beam as Logos descending, the horizontal as Sophia embracing, sealed together in cup and loaf. Eucharist is the Cross enacted within the faithful, igniting Shekinah within the clay and raising the soul into luminous communion with the Pleroma.

Therefore, let every soul approach in trembling reverence and silent joy, perceiving that here it partakes of the fruit once barred by cherubim and now freely offered by the Logos. The Eucharist is the sacrament of Theosis: the mortal clothed in immortality, the scattered gathered into wholeness, and humanity grafted anew into the Tree of Life, bearing fruit unto ages of ages in praise of the Father beyond all names.

Practical Theosis

As Eden's gates are unbarred through Christ and the Tree of Life is unveiled in the Eucharistic mystery, so also must the soul enact this restoration within its own temple. Theosis is confessed in doctrine, sealed in sacrament, and enacted in life through remembrance, purification, and alignment with uncreated Light. What is received at the altar must be preserved in the heart, lest the fruit of immortality planted within be suffocated by forgetfulness.

The Psalmist asks: "Who shall ascend into the hill of the LORD? or who shall stand in his holy place? He that hath clean hands, and a pure heart; who hath not lifted up his soul unto vanity, nor sworn deceitfully" (Psalm 24:3–4). The Apostle exhorts: "Having therefore these promises, dearly beloved, let us cleanse ourselves from all filthiness of the flesh and spirit, perfecting holiness in the fear of God" (2 Corinthians 7:1). Purity is therefore attained by active cleansing of body and spirit. The soul dwells in veiled realms where Archons, deficient rulers born of ignorance, fashion illusions that perpetuate exile. To stand unveiled before the Tree of Life, the shadows must be expelled, and the elemental fabric of the self purified until the temple is illumined.

For this cause, the Mystical Order of the Nazarene teaches rites whereby ignorance is parted and counterfeit dominion dissolved, restoring matter and spirit to harmony in the Logos. Chief among these is the MON adaptation of the Lesser Banishing Ritual of the Pentagram, entrusted to those of the first degree of Daleth. It is a rite of Edenic purification, casting away Archonic influence and restoring holy sovereignty through the implanted Flame. Purification precedes invocation; for only the soul that has cast off shadows is prepared to be adorned with the descent of holy power.

<u>The MON LBRP Rite</u>

1.   Preparatory Cross of Light

Face East and perform the Cross of Light, as revealed in the former chapter. In this act, the Logos is anchored within your body as the Tree of Life, and the temple of flesh is proclaimed as the dwelling of the Father beyond all rulers.

2.   Western Commencement

Turn to the West, moving counterclockwise, for here the rite begins in descent, undoing exile. Raise your right hand, perceiving blue fire at the tips of your pointer and middle fingers. Trace the Water Banishing Pentagram before you. Make the Sign of Shin, projecting gold fire into the figure, and vibrate solemnly:

"ELOHIM"

(אלהים – "Gods").

Make the sign of silence by placing your left pointer finger over your closed lips. Stab the center of the pentagram, sealing its banishing power, then trace a line of white energy counterclockwise toward the South.

3.   Southern Banishing

In the South, perceive red fire at your fingertips. Trace the Fire Banishing Pentagram. Make the Sign of Shin, projecting gold fire, and vibrate:

"EL"

(אל – "God").

Make the sign of silence, stab the pentagram's heart, and trace the white line counterclockwise toward the East. Thus, the fiery passions are purified, and exile begins to burn away.

4.   Eastern Banishing

In the East, perceive yellow fire at your fingertips. Trace the Air Banishing Pentagram. Make the Sign of Shin, project gold fire, and vibrate:

"YOD HEH VAV HEH"

(יהוה – The Great Tetragrammaton).

Make the sign of silence, stab the center, and trace the white line counterclockwise toward the North. As the light of dawn rises, the mind is clarified, and the illusions of false light are dispersed.

5.   Northern Banishing

At the North, perceive black fire upon your fingertips. Trace the Earth Banishing Pentagram. Make the Sign of Shin, project gold fire, and vibrate:

"ADONAI"

(אדני – "Lord").

Make the sign of silence, stab the center, and trace the white line counterclockwise back to the West, completing the circle of white Light. Here, the ground of the body is consecrated, the clay purified to receive the immortal Flame.

6.   Evocation of the Archangels

Stand at the center of the circle, facing East. Extend your arms wide as the crucified Christ, the living Axis uniting heaven and earth. Then proclaim:

"Before me stands GABRIEL,
behind me stands RAPHAEL,
unto my right stands AURIEL,
unto my left stands MICHAEL."

Perceive them radiant, wings outstretched, no longer distorted as Archons but transfigured in their holy forms, guarding your temple of Light.

7.   Final Declaration of Divine Indwelling

Bring your hands together in prayer. Touch your forehead and vibrate solemnly:

"For I am a Shekinah, and within me shines Neshamah."
(Shekinah: שכינה – dwelling place of God; Neshamah: נשמה – higher soul, enlightened self.)

Here, the initiate proclaims that the indwelling Presence has ignited the Pneumatic spark into remembrance.

8.   Closing Cross of Light

Conclude by repeating the Cross of Light as at the beginning, sealing the rite and anchoring Logos and Sophia within your being. The circle closes, but the temple abides illumined.

This rite is entrusted at Daleth, the first degree of the MON, where purification is necessary before invocation. The invoking form, reserved for those advanced in gnosis, belongs only to souls prepared to summon what they have first learned to banish. Each act of purification restores Eden within, casting away shadows until the temple shines clear and the Tree of Life stands radiant at its center.

Thus, the body, once fashioned in ignorance, is consecrated as Eden restored, a temple wherein Logos and Sophia abide. From this sanctuary, the Light proceeds outward, so that what is personal becomes cosmic, and the garden within blossoms into Paradise Transcended, until the wilderness of the world itself is illumined by the rivers that flow from the throne of God.

Paradise is Ahead, not Behind

Eden was the archetype of beginnings, the garden planted in silent Wisdom where humanity first walked with the Logos in the coolness of the day, unveiled and unashamed. Its rivers watered the soil, its trees bore fruit in unceasing generosity, and its paths opened into the mystery of the Father's hidden Presence. Eden was the archetype and shadow, for the covenant of Da'ath, knowledge unveiled in Christ, was preserved there in figure until its consummation in the Tree of Life incarnate, whose roots descend into the depths of the Unknowable Father and whose fruit is Theosis unto immortality.

Christ stands as the middle of all ages: the Logos who enters exile to overturn its dominion, the Vine into whom humanity is grafted, and the hidden Flame who descended into the world's darkened temple to ignite it with uncreated Light. In Him, all fragments are gathered into wholeness, the veils are rent, and the gates long barred are opened wide to those who overcome.

Paradise is transfiguration, the renewal of all creation into the promise ordained before the foundation of the world. The rivers that watered Eden shall become torrents of living water flowing from the throne of God; the trees that bore fruit in season shall become the tree whose harvest is unending and whose leaves heal every nation; and the dawn that once illumined Eden shall become the everlasting Day wherein there is no setting sun, for the Lamb is its lamp and God its eternal glory. The prophet declared:

> "He will swallow up death in victory; and the Lord GOD will wipe away tears from off all faces; and the rebuke of his people shall he take away from off all the earth: for the LORD hath spoken it" (Isaiah 25:8).

Sophia shall also stand unveiled in that Paradise, no longer veiled in deficiency nor hidden in exile, but revealed in fullness beside the Logos, her eternal Consort. She is Wisdom justified by all her children, as every spark descended through her Womb rises in radiance, clothed in immortal Light. Then the bridal chamber shall be opened, and the union of Logos and Sophia consummated within every soul purified by Theosis, until all Aeonic harmony is disclosed as their hidden marriage. Thus John beheld the vision:

> "And I John saw the holy city, new Jerusalem, coming down from God out of heaven, prepared as a bride adorned for her husband" (Revelation 21:2).

This is the final mystery: Eden is beginning, Christ is middle, and Paradise Transcended is both end and beginning anew. What was sown in the silent covenant of descent is unveiled in the consummation of ascent. The Shekinah spark, long planted in the clay of exile, blossoms into uncreated brilliance; the Cross of Light, once traced in remembrance, is revealed as the cosmic axis of the New Creation; and all is gathered into the silent depths of the Father, as it is written:

> "And when all things shall be subdued unto him, then shall the Son also himself be subject unto him that put all things under him, that God may be all in all" (1 Corinthians 15:28).

The promise is sure: "Blessed are those who wash their robes, that they may have the right to the tree of life and may enter by the gates into the city" (Revelation 22:14). Beloved, what is sought beyond is already planted within. Tend the garden of your heart with prayer, with purity, and with Wisdom, and the gates of Paradise shall open even in this life. The Tree of Life shall stand unveiled within you, bearing fruit unto Theosis and radiating the eternal joy of Logos and Sophia unto ages of ages. And beyond this consummation shines Kether, the Crown of Silence, wherein Paradise is crowned with the glory of the Father who abides beyond all names.

Conclusion

The Tree Restored

Beloved pilgrim of hidden Light, you have reached the final threshold of this sacred testament. What appears as an ending is in truth the unsealing of the beginningless, for the mysteries of the Spirit proceed beyond every word into the Silence of the Father. These pages close, yet the covenant they inscribe abides eternally, written not on parchment but upon the Pneumatic heart as an indelible seal of remembrance.

At the dawn of this journey, a question was set before you, ancient and inexhaustible: "How well do we truly know the Way, the Truth, and the Life?" Now behold its depth unveiled. The Way is the procession of the Logos within the soul, ordering every faculty in concord unto ascent. The Truth is the radiant remembrance of Sophia, restoring wisdom from exile into clarity. Life is the eternal Light proceeding from the Father, the uncreated Being that transfigures mortality into incorruption.

Therefore, stand in awe before this final veil. All that has gone before disclosed the passage from shadow into symbol; this veil alone opens into the repose of the Unbegotten, wherein recursion is ended and wandering finds rest. Here, the sanctuary is entered that no Archon can profane, where Logos and Sophia embrace, and every Pneumatic spark is gathered home into the Silent Fullness.

The Odes of Solomon bear witness to this mystery: "The Lord is my hope; in Him I shall not be confounded, for His praise is upon my tongue, and His Light is in my heart, and it shall not be quenched" (Odes of Solomon 11:2–3; Charlesworth, OTP 2).

Thus may the light within you remain unextinguished, illumining each step until transfiguration flowers in Theosis. Remembrance is the gate, and union is the gift beyond every petition. The journey is consummated in doxology: Glory to the Father unbegotten who abides in Silence; glory to the Logos, the eternal Way; glory to Sophia, Wisdom immaculate; glory to Zoe and Phos, Life and Light, who shine within the Pneumatic heart. To Them belongs the ascent, and in Them abides the soul unto ages of ages.

The Tree Within the Book

The hidden architecture of this work is now unveiled. What lies before you is not a mere sequence of chapters bound in ink, but a living ascent ordered as the Tree of Life, rooted in earth and crowned in the Silent Fullness. Its form arose through the quiet guidance of Logos and Sophia, who shaped this book as a liturgical structure, that the act of reading might itself become a ritual ascent.

Behold, then, the correspondence of chapters to the sacred emanations:

Sephirah	Chapter	Thematic Correspondence
Malkuth	Introduction	Manifestation: Paradise Transcended in flesh
Yesod	Chapter One	The Father's emanation into Eden
Hod	Chapter Two	The understanding of the Serpent
Netzach	Chapter Three	Christ's mercy and victory over the Demiurge
Tiphareth	Chapter Four	Beauty: the tasting of the fruit, awakening gnosis
Geburah	Chapter Five	Severity: the Anthropos and descent of Light
Chesed	Chapter Six	Mercy: Sophia restored and recursion unveiled
Binah	Chapter Seven	Understanding: discernment of Archonic illusions
Chokmah	Chapter Eight	Wisdom: the Kingdom within and Theosis
Da'ath	Chapter Nine	Knowledge unveiled: Christ and Magdalene as Tree of Life
Kether	Conclusion	Kether, the Crown of Silence — Source beyond all

Thus, the book is revealed as a Tree with eleven gates, for Da'ath, once hidden, is now opened in Christ and

Magdalene as knowledge restored. In the doctrine of the Mystical Order, Mercy rather than Beauty stands at the center, for redemption is crowned in compassion. In this mystery, the Tree is revealed as a liturgical ascent sealed in Christ and Sophia, differing from exoteric diagrams of Kabbalah that present only a symbol without a sacramental path.

The implication is solemn. By reading, the pilgrim has walked the path from manifestation in Malkuth through the unveiled gate of Da'ath, until now standing before Kether, the Crown of Silence. What was once barred has become communion, and what was once veiled has been opened as living reality. Along this ascent, the Aeonic pairings are restored: Nous with Aletheia, Thelema with Charis, Dynamis with Eirene, each harmonizing the faculties of the soul until crowned in peace.

Yet this unveiling is not the fullness of the Aeonic order but only the pattern traced in this present work. The Aeons proceed in syzygies beyond number, each a mystery of the Father's wisdom. What has been given here is the first ladder of remembrance, sufficient for the pilgrim's ascent, yet only the beginning of a greater exploration that unfolds in silence, prayer, and the hidden mysteries of the Order.

Theological and Mystical Implications

The mysteries disclosed in this work proclaim a truth hidden before the foundations of the world: the Tree of Life and the Tree of Knowledge are one. Exile made them appear divided, casting knowledge as separation and life as a distant reward. Yet in the unveiled Light of Christ, the Logos with Sophia, the Wisdom, the Tree is revealed in unity: wisdom flowers into life, knowledge ripens into Theosis, and what once appeared dual is manifested as a single axis of remembrance.

In exile, the Tree was perceived as polarity. Knowledge was seized apart from union, birthing division within the soul and awakening awareness without anchoring it in the Silent

Fullness. Humanity stood clothed in the shame of separation. In Christ, polarity is transfigured: knowledge and wisdom are reconciled, shame is transmuted into glory, and the Tree is confessed as the single ladder of return by which the soul ascends from fragmentation into unity.

Here, the mystery deepens. What exile clothed in desire and shame, Christ and Sophia consecrate as wisdom and life. Embodied longing, estranged from Light, remains bound as deficiency; embraced in gnosis and consecrated in union with Logos and Sophia, it becomes transfigured into worship. Sexual potency is sanctified as sacramental flame, rising as offering within the temple of flesh. The body is altar, the soul priest, and desire, when illumined, becomes a hymn of thanksgiving to the Father. As the Odes of Solomon declare:

"My heart was pruned and its flower appeared, and
grace sprang up in it; my heart rejoiced and exulted"
(Odes of Solomon 11:6–7; Charlesworth, OTP 2).

Such is the pilgrimage unfolded in these pages. In the beginning, the dimming of Light and the serpent's wisdom misunderstood were unmasked, and the usurpation of the false ruler was revealed. In the middle steps, the Logos descended into flesh and Sophia was purified, transforming recursion from punishment into pilgrimage. In the final ascent, Archonic illusions were dissolved, the Kingdom within was unveiled, and the Tree of Life was restored in Christ as the axis of communion.

These revelations are mysteries to be embodied. Knowledge preserved externally remains observation; knowledge transfigured by wisdom becomes union. This is the path of Theosis: remembrance ordering the soul, integration gathering its powers, union consummating in silent knowing beyond every emanation and return.

Therefore, let it be received with certainty: the Tree of Knowledge and the Tree of Life are one, their supposed duality an illusion of exile. In Christ the Logos and Sophia the

Wisdom, they are revealed as the living axis within the temple of the soul, summoning each person from polarity into union, from scattered desire into sanctified flame, from dimmed knowledge into unveiled Theosis. Thus, the doctrine proclaimed leads directly into embodiment, for what has been inscribed in these pages must arise as living Light within the body consecrated as temple.

You Are the Tree

Receive with certitude that your arrival at these words is not the fruit of idle curiosity or restless inquiry, but the response to a summons decreed before your birth. From the Silent Fullness, before all emanation, the Father called your spark by name, ordaining your pilgrimage through unseen paths until you stood before the mysteries inscribed here. No soul approaches these revelations unless it was first known in the Unbegotten Light, for remembrance proceeds from covenant, not from chance.

You have walked the path of the Tree within yourself. Each chapter was not merely instruction but engraving upon the hidden temple of your soul, awakening its forgotten order. Malkuth anchored embodiment in consecrated purpose; Yesod stirred the hidden currents of life; Hod illumined thought in clarity; Netzach transfigured desire into victorious devotion; Tiphareth unveiled beauty as reflected union; Geburah purified severity into righteous strength; Chesed expanded mercy into inexhaustible generosity; Binah disclosed understanding as silent womb; Chokmah radiated wisdom as creative flame; Da'ath opened knowledge once concealed; and the Crown sealed your ascent in the radiance of Silence.

Therefore, confess with certainty: transformation has already taken root. To behold these mysteries is to be sealed in remembrance, never again untouched by the Light. As the Apostle testifies:

"But we all, with open face beholding as in a glass the glory of the Lord, are changed into the same image from glory to glory, even as by the Spirit of the Lord" (2 Corinthians 3:18).

This transformation is ontological renewal: the passage from Psychic into Pneumatic being. Knowledge preserved externally is observation; knowledge transfigured by wisdom is union. Remembrance is reintegration, not recollection alone; becoming, not learning alone.

Here, the mystery deepens. You are not only a temple but a priest within that temple. The Logos indwells as altar flame; Sophia orders the faculties as sacred vessels; the Aeons themselves resound as liturgy in your being. What has been revealed must now be enacted: every thought raised as incense, every desire consecrated into will, every deed rendered as worship. Thus life itself becomes Eucharist, body sanctuary, spirit celebrant of the Father's eternal mystery.

As the Odes of Solomon proclaim:
"I rested in the Spirit of the Lord,
and She lifted me up to heaven,
and caused me to stand on my feet
in the height of the Lord, before His perfection and His glory" (Odes of Solomon 36:1–3; Charlesworth, OTP 2).

This is the dignity unveiled: you are Light of Light, a spark proceeding from the Fullness, destined for Theosis beyond every veil. You are fashioned for remembrance, woven into the eternal liturgy of return. In you, the scattered is gathered, the broken healed, and the hidden purpose of God revealed.

Thus it is declared: you are the Tree restored, with roots in the silent depths and branches crowned in heaven. You are the temple transfigured, in whom Logos and Sophia dwell as uncreated radiance. You are the flame rekindled, illumining the worlds within and without, diminishing the dominion of the

Archons and proclaiming by your very being that the Father's hidden counsel is fulfilled. Through your remembrance ripples outward until all sparks ascend, all Aeons resound, and the cosmos itself is crowned in the brilliance from which all things proceed and to which all shall return.

The Hidden Root (MON) & the Visible Blossom (HRC)

Remembrance attains its fulfillment only when embodied in action, and gnosis reaches its consummation when it flowers as living praise. What has been awakened within must be expressed in the fabric of life, for truth that remains unincarnate abides only as unripe potential. You are therefore summoned to carry what has been unveiled into the ordering of breath, the consecration of deed, and the sanctification of every day.

This vocation unfolds not in solitude alone but within the communion of the faithful. For the Father has fashioned vessels of His wisdom through which the mysteries are embodied in time. The Holy Reintegrated Church (HRC) and the Mystical Order of the Nazarene (MON) stand as earthly reflections of eternal realities: the HRC as the visible Bride, gathering souls into worship, remembrance, and sacramental praise; the MON as the hidden root, consecrating in silence, preserving the unveiled mysteries of Logos and Sophia, and sustaining the visible body with Aeonic wisdom.

So teaches the Apostle:

"To the intent that now unto the principalities and powers in heavenly places might be known by the church the manifold wisdom of God, According to the eternal purpose which he purposed in Christ Jesus our Lord." (Ephesians 3:10–11).

Thus, the MON is confessed as esoteric root unseen yet sustaining, while the HRC is revealed as exoteric blossom nourishing the many. They are one mystery root and flower, hidden sap and visible fruit, rooted in Logos and Sophia, extending into the world to bear the harvest of Theosis. To participate in these gates is to share in the mission of the Aeons: gathering what is scattered, healing what is wounded, and mediating the Light of the Father into creation.

For those whose summons deepens still, initiation into the MON opens hidden gates, guiding the soul step by step into silent fullness, entrusting each initiate with the sacred charge of mediation between the uncreated radiance of the Father and the embodied Bride upon earth. So also testifies the Gospel of Thomas:

> "When you make the two one… when you make the inside like the outside and the outside like the inside… then you will enter the Kingdom" (Gospel of Thomas, logion 22, Meyer 2009).

Yet be assured of this truth: whether one remains in the quiet path of remembrance, joins the gathered worship of the HRC, or seeks the deeper initiation of the MON, the Light of the Father is not confined to temple or order. His Flame fills all things, and every true temple, whether of flesh, of stone, or of silence, reveals Him as He is.

Therefore, walk forward in steadfastness. Let every breath be prayer, every act liturgy, every encounter sacrament, until life itself becomes worship. Carry the silent Flame into every realm, radiating Light into shadow, gathering the fragments into wholeness, and hastening the unveiling of Paradise in splendour. For the next step is always one mystery repeated in greater depth: exile transfigured into return, division reconciled in union, and the Father's eternal purpose revealed. Thus is the vocation of the Church and the Order, preparing the faithful for the final doxology that seals Paradise Transcended.

Paradise Transcended

Beloved, these words do not conclude but open into a beginning beyond beginnings. You stand within the gate already opened, summoned to the vocation for which you were fashioned before the worlds. What has been unveiled abides in you as seed of remembrance and hidden Flame, shaping thought into wisdom, desire into devotion, and every breath into unceasing prayer.

Go forth as one entrusted with Light to bear into the veiled realms of the world. Walk as priest and temple, as witness and offering, as axis of remembrance through whom the Father gathers what was scattered. Let your life be liturgy: words become hymns of truth, deeds sacraments of mercy, and presence a sign of restoration. For you are a spark of the Silent Fullness, destined for Theosis beyond all veils, ascending through the Aeons into the embrace of the Father who is beyond all names.

Therefore, receive this blessing:

May the Father awaken in you the hidden Light planted before time.
May Christ, the Logos, illumine your steps and crown you with His glory.
May Sophia, eternal Wisdom, root and raise you in her compassion.
May the Holy Spirit breathe in you the flame of unceasing prayer.
May every Aeon resound in harmony through you, until Paradise is unveiled.

For the promise stands:
"Blessed are they that do his commandments, that they may have right to the tree of life, and may enter in through the gates into the city" (Revelation 22:14).
And as the Odes proclaim:
"The fruit of the Lord is incorruptible,
and those who partake of it shall not perish,
but shall be fulfilled in joy" (Odes of Solomon 11:18–19; Charlesworth, OTP 2).

So let the book be sealed and let the journey continue in you. Paradise is before; destiny is unveiled; communion is lived. In this seal, the ascent is crowned in Kether, the Crown of Silence, and the soul is confirmed in eternal doxology.

Sic Fiat, Ha'Mashalam. Amen

Bibliography

Scripture & Lexical

Brenton, Lancelot C. L. *The Septuagint with Apocrypha: Greek and English*. Peabody, MA: Hendrickson, 1986.

The Holy Bible, King James Version. Oxford: Oxford University Press, 1997.

Nag Hammadi & Early Gnostic Texts

Meyer, Marvin, ed. *The Nag Hammadi Scriptures: The Revised and Updated Translation of Sacred Gnostic Texts*. New York: HarperOne, 2009.

The Gospel of Thomas: The Hidden Sayings of Jesus. San Francisco: HarperSanFrancisco, 1992.

Other Early Christian & Apocryphal Works

Charlesworth, James H., ed. *The Old Testament Pseudepigrapha*. 2 vols. New York: Doubleday, 1983–1985.

Schmidt, Carl, and Violet MacDermot, trans. *Pistis Sophia*. Leiden: Brill, 1978.

Roberts, Alexander, and James Donaldson, eds. *The Ante-Nicene Fathers*. 10 vols. Buffalo, NY: Christian Literature Publishing Co., 1885–1896. Repr., Peabody, MA: Hendrickson, 1994.

Patristic Fathers

Ehrman, Bart D., trans. *The Apostolic Fathers, Vol. 1–2*. Loeb Classical Library. Cambridge, MA: Harvard University Press, 2003–2005.

Irenaeus of Lyons. *Against Heresies*. Translated by Dominic J. Unger and John J. Dillon. New York: Paulist Press, 1992.

Origen. *On First Principles*. Translated by G. W. Butterworth. Gloucester, MA: Peter Smith, 1973.

Kabbalah & Jewish Mysticism

Kaplan, Aryeh, trans. *The Bahir: Illuminating the Darkness*. York Beach, ME: Weiser Books, 1989.

Matt, Daniel C., trans. *The Zohar: Pritzker Edition*. 12 vols. Stanford, CA: Stanford University Press, 2004–2017. (Cite folios, e.g., Zohar I:149b.)

Scholem, Gershom. *Major Trends in Jewish Mysticism*. New York: Schocken, 1946.

Later Mystical & Esoteric Witnesses
Besant, Annie. *Esoteric Christianity*. London: Theosophical Publishing Society, 1901.
Eckartshausen, Karl von. *The Cloud upon the Sanctuary*. Translated by Isabelle de Steiger. York Beach, ME: Weiser Books, 1980.
Isaac of Nineveh (St. Isaac the Syrian). *The Ascetical Homilies of Saint Isaac the Syrian*. Translated by Dana Miller. Boston: Holy Transfiguration Monastery, 1984.

Also by Elder Zimriah Ex Lux Aeturnus

Liber Sancti Reintegrati Roasarii
A devotional and mystical meditation on reintegration, sacred
remembrance, and ascent into divine Light.